Merry Christmas
Mommy

Brittany XOXOX

John XoXoX

12/25/04

PRESENTED TO:

_____

FROM:

_____

DATE:

_____

CHRISTMAS

CELEBRATING THE JOY OF FAITH AND FAMILY...

GOD'S WAY

WHITE STONE BOOKS
LAKELAND, FLORIDA

07 06 05 04   10 9 8 7 6 5 4 3 2 1

CHRISTMAS—CELEBRATING THE JOY OF FAITH AND FAMILY...GOD'S WAY
ISBN 1-59379-019-5
COPYRIGHT © 2004 JOHN M. THURBER
THURBER CREATIVE SERVICES, INC.
TULSA, OKLAHOMA

EDITORIAL DEVELOPMENT AND LITERARY REPRESENTATION BY
MARK GILROY COMMUNICATIONS, INC.
6528 E. 101ST STREET, SUITE 416
TULSA, OKLAHOMA 74133-6754

PUBLISHED BY WHITE STONE BOOKS
P.O. BOX 2835
LAKELAND, FLORIDA 33806

$\mathcal{I}$NTRODUCTION

"For I know the plans I have for you," declares the LORD, "plans to prosper you
and not to harm you, plans to give you hope and a future."

JEREMIAH 29:11 NIV

God is faithfully at work today in the lives of families and individuals all around the world—revealing His purpose, demonstrating His awesome power, and expressing His infinite love.

In today's busy lifestyle, more than ever we need that tangible assurance of God's glorious presence and His enduring love.

Maybe you are seeking hope and encouragement this holiday season. Perhaps you are simply looking to strengthen and renew your faith.

God's Way for Christmas is filled with true and tender holiday stories—real life reminders that Christmas truly begins in the loving heart of the Father.

Are you ready to encounter this upcoming holiday season in a brand-new way? Now is your moment to experience Christmas in your heart anew—God's magnificent and beautiful gift to the world, His Son.

CONTENTS

CHRISTMAS

CELEBRATING THE JOY OF FAITH AND FAMILY...

GOD'S WAY

$\mathcal{J}$ULIE

AMANDA PILGRIM

Come now, and let us reason together, saith the LORD:

though your sins be as scarlet, they shall be as white as snow;

though they be red like crimson, they shall be as wool.

ISAIAH 1:18

Money was tight at our house the year my parents divorced. My mother immediately began to worry about Christmas and how she was going to be able to buy any presents. It was tough being a single mother with no outside help. She had to take on a third job painting Christmas designs on storefront windows just to try to make ends meet, much less have any hope of buying a Christmas present for her three-year-old daughter.

Disappointed that she couldn't buy me a Christmas present, she took out some old cloth and yarn and decided to make me one instead. She worked long into the nights sewing, stitching, and embroidering.

"THE BLESSING OF AN EARTHLY FAMILY GIVES US ONLY A HAZY PICTURE OF THE BLESSING IN GOD'S HEAVENLY FAMILY."

—*Janette Oke*

Three weeks later, Christmas morning found this little girl bouncing out of bed and running to the tree to find the treasures that might be there waiting to be discovered.

My mother stood and watched with hesitant apprehension to see if I would like the doll she had worked so feverishly on. She was ashamed that she had not been able to buy a store-bought doll with frilly dresses and long silky hair. All she had been able to provide for her little girl was a homemade doll with yellow yarn hair and a face that had been hand embroidered.

There sat the doll, blonde hair, big blue eyes, and a beautiful pink frilly dress. Without hesitation, I dashed over and gathered her up into my arms. My mother's eyes filled with tears as I joyfully named her "Julie!"

Years later as I prepared to marry and move away, Julie was carefully packed into a box and placed in the storage shed with the last of my belongings. When I came home to get the remaining boxes, my heart filled with anguish as I looked down at the treasure I had held dear for so many years. Over those few months I had been away, rain had seeped into the shed, and Julie was covered in black mold. Her face, body, and dress were ruined!

Everyone said that there was nothing that could be done to save my precious Julie doll. They told me it would be best if I just threw her away, but I just couldn't do it. Julie had given me so much joy through the years. With tears in my eyes I went to my mother, the maker of my precious treasure.

My mother took Julie carefully in her hands and apprehensively inspected her—I went home, my heart full of sadness as I recalled the years of happiness Julie had given me.

A few weeks later as our family gathered together for Christmas, I unwrapped a very special gift from my mother. Julie was inside! Bright, clean, and smiling Julie! My mother had done it! When everyone else said nothing could be done and the doll was ruined, my mother had not given up. With unrelenting determination she had worked hour upon hour fixing Julie and making her like new again.

I often think of my Julie doll when I look at people— especially the ones that society might say are ruined, that there is no hope for them, and it would be best to simply move on and forget about them.

It is then that I am reminded of my Heavenly Father who is the Master of restoration. He created each of us with a specifically designed plan and can, in an instant, make us like new again. Best of all, He doesn't give up on anyone.

Julie has now been with me for twenty-four years. She sits on a shelf above my bed. And after years of store-bought dolls and fancy dresses, Julie is still my most prized possession and a constant reminder of a loving Father who will never give up on me.

*O*UR SEASON OF FAITH

HUGH CHAPMAN

That if thou shalt confess with thy mouth the Lord Jesus,

and shalt believe in thine heart that God hath

raised him from the dead, thou shalt be saved.

R O M A N S   1 0 : 9

Though my career as a banker was financially rewarding, I was never quite content with the work. Compliance regulations, qualification formulas, and credit declinations always seemed so cold and, well…calculating. It was no wonder that, after only my fourth year on the job, I began to look with envy at the teaching career my wife, Julie, had chosen. Still, to make a career move so late in my life seemed absolutely out of the question. To leave a secure position and return to school was something that would take more faith (and throwing more caution to the wind) than I possessed.

Yet God continued to speak to me through an odd feeling of longing that would often ease into my deliberation. I'd find myself watching Julie as she graded papers until late at night. In the soft lamplight I'd see her smile with satisfaction at the progress of her students and sigh with dismay when they failed to meet her expectations. Though her salary was only half the amount of mine, I knew she was much more gratified in her career than I had ever been. And in time, I began to realize that there must be something more to teaching than I was able to see.

Then one winter evening I found her fretting, in typical fourth-grade teacher fashion, over a student's worsening academic performance. "Baxter will never be a strong student," she said with a sigh, "but at least he used to try. He began the year doing so well, but now his work has dropped to nearly nothing. I just don't understand it."

Two days later the answer became very clear—for both of us.

That evening as I arrived home, exhausted from a hard day at the office, Julie met me at the doorway. "Will you drive me to Baxter's house?" she asked.

I looked at my watch in dismay. It was already getting dark. "Oh, I don't want to bother strangers this late," I whined, "and besides, it's cold out there." But Julie was adamant and promised that she only wanted to drive by to see the house. Reluctantly, I agreed, and together we began our journey.

Baxter's home was at least twenty miles from where we lived, but more than just the distance, the place was hard to find in the dark. We turned off the highway, and then rumbled down a rural Arkansas county roadway with only a vague notion as to where we were going. In time, we turned from the graveled road onto a narrow dirt path. My concern was growing by the minute. "You know, some of these folks have shotguns by the door," I said, "and they don't always welcome strangers in the middle of the night."

But my wife was determined. "It's only six o'clock," she said, "and besides, it can't be much farther." Then pointing excitedly, she said, "Look, there it is."

Before us stood an old run-down trailer house, unlit and barely visible in the mid-winter darkness. In what might have been called a front yard (which was really only a cleared spot in the woods) there were four elementary-aged children. Some were bundled in jackets, others in only their shirtsleeves. Two were busily gathering firewood, one was pouring kerosene into a lantern, and another was petting a mangy old dog. As we pulled slowly forward, a chubby kid in overalls hurried toward the car and enthusiastically greeted Julie. "My mom's not home yet, Mrs. Chapman, so you can't come in. But we can visit out here."

And though my wife did happily chat with the boy for ten minutes, there was really no need to go inside. She had seen what she had come to see; the run-down dwelling of her fourth-grade student and all his siblings—heated with a tiny wood stove and illuminated with two kerosene lamps.

On the quiet drive home, Julie batted back a tear as she softly verbalized what we both had witnessed. "His work was good in the early fall when the days were longer. But now that it gets dark so early, he can't see to do his homework." It was then that I began to understand what she had known all along. Within her classroom my wife had worked to find a means to reach these children—and perhaps to even release them from a life of destitution.

As I drove through the Arkansas night, I watched her from the corner of my eye, and from deep within I realized that I, too, had discovered what God was calling me to do. The only question that remained was whether or not I had the faith to make the change.

What I hadn't counted on was that God had been speaking to Julie, too, and as we discussed the possibilities—tentatively at first, then later more boldly—we began to formulate a plan. By the end of the month, I had said farewell to my friends at the bank.

Then for two and a half years we struggled to make ends meet while I attended college. Eventually, our perseverance paid off, and I was offered my first contract.

I would teach junior high special education in the same district that my wife had been teaching fourth grade.

After my first day I proudly brought forth my new class roster for Julie to see. There among the list of seventh graders was a name that we both recognized: my wife's former student, Baxter. He had found the strength to hang on, and had finally made it into junior high—and so had I.

As we began our new venture together, Baxter and I became fast friends. He was a big friendly kid with a permanently fixed smile, and though his ability was well below many of his classmates, he always gave his very best.

It was disheartening to watch him struggle so hard and to produce so little. One evening I shared my dismay with Julie.

"It seems so unfair," I said. "Baxter struggles every day, and I can't seem to help him much. I'm thinking that maybe a more experienced teacher could do a better job."

Julie softly shook her head and replied with a sympathetic smile. "God put you in that classroom with Baxter for a purpose. You might not be able to see it now, but someday you will. You just have to have faith and hang in there."

Her words were encouraging, but I'm afraid her faith was greater than mine. Then something strange happened.

It was nearing Christmastime of that first year, and in the excitement of the upcoming vacation, I was having a hard time keeping the attention of my class. In hopes of making the most of an unruly situation, I assigned an essay: "What Christmas Means to Me."

It was then that Baxter surprised me with his composition.

Though short and ill arranged, it represented, for him, a massive effort. In large block-printed letters and with writing seasoned in a jumble of spelling and punctuation errors, the sincerity of his work was shining through.

WHAT CHRISTMAS MEANS TO ME

Some wise men heard that a new king would be born in Bethlehem, and they made their way through the woods to find Him and they followed a star and they came to a barn where the baby was already born. And when they saw Him, they knew it was Jesus, and they

bowed down and worshiped Him, because they knew
that the new baby lying in a manger would be the King
of all kings.

I looked to Baxter with a newfound respect as he stood beside my desk waiting, hopefully, for my approval. When I paused to gather my thoughts Baxter quickly pointed out, "There's more on the back."

Pleasantly surprised at the length and the relative accuracy of his effort, I quickly turned over the page to read the conclusion of Baxter's essay.

The wise men were amazed at all they had seen that
night, and while they were walking back to their homes,
they talked about all the great things they had
seen. Then, when they got about halfway home, one of
the wise men turned to the others and said, "Hey, do you
know what? This ought to be a Holiday." And from then
on, it was.

Baxter remained at my desk with his simple, friendly smile.

He was not trying to be cute, nor funny, nor insincere.

He was simply reporting an important event in the way he had imagined it to be. And for his honesty, I admired him all the more.

"Baxter," I asked, "do you believe that? Do you believe that Jesus is the Son of God, and that He was sent here to be our Savior?"

Baxter seemed uncomfortable and shifted his weight from one foot to another. Finally he said, "I'm not sure, Mr. Chapman. I go to church sometimes, and that's what they say. But how can you know something like that for sure?"

"You have to have faith that it's true, Bax," I said, pointing to my chest. "And when you have faith, you'll know, because you'll feel it deep inside your heart."

He looked solemnly toward me. "Do you believe it?" he asked.

I nodded assuredly. "I do, Baxter, and very much so."

My student then smiled happily. "Well, if you believe it, then I believe it, too, Mr. Chapman. Because you're real smart, and you know almost everything."

From deep within, I felt his sincerity, but I had to shake my head. "No, Baxter. You shouldn't believe it because I believe it; you should believe it because you feel it from deep within your own heart. That's how you'll know for sure."

As Baxter walked away that day, I experienced a new feeling of purpose, one that I had not known before that moment.

And from my own heart, I knew that I was exactly where God intended for me to be.

It was six weeks later, shortly after the kids returned from Christmas vacation, that Baxter approached my desk.

This time he held a small New Testament, open to a well-marked page with a single underlined verse: "For God so loved the world, that he gave his only begotten Son, that whosoever believeth in Him should not perish, but have everlasting life."

Excitedly he whispered, "They gave this to me at church, Mr. Chapman, on the day I was saved. They say I can keep it for my own."

Though I shook Baxter's hand and patted his back, there was no way I could express the happiness I felt for the decision he had made.

⋘

More than a decade has passed since Baxter entered my first classroom. As a now-seasoned teacher, I've learned that students come suddenly into our care, share a part of our lives, and then often just as quickly, they move on to other things. Occasionally, however, through our time together, our lives are altered forever.

Two years ago at Thanksgiving my family received word that Baxter had been in an automobile accident. Police reports indicated no drinking, no drugs, and no hazardous road conditions—just a single automobile with a single fatality on a quiet, Arkansas highway.

I said a prayer that day for Baxter, but I knew that the important decision had been made long before; an arrangement born of faith within the trusting heart of a determined young man.

Sometimes even now, in the quiet of an early winter's evening, I'll find myself driving along winding country roads. And I'll recall how a boy named Baxter, who through his own faith, exchanged a broken-down trailer house for a mansion on high.

And from deep within my heart I hold to my own faith, the assurance that I will see him again one day; only this time it will be in the company of the King of kings.

And you know what?

A day like that just ought to be a Holiday.

ℛOOM IN THE INN

TEENA M. STEWART

For I was hungry and you gave me something to eat,

I was thirsty and you gave me something to drink,

I was a stranger and you invited me in, I needed clothes

and you clothed me, I was sick and you looked after me,

I was in prison and you came to visit me...whatever you did

for one of the least of these brothers of mine, you did for me.

MATTHEW 25:35-36,40 NIV

"I got something really special at the store when I was Christmas shopping," said Janis that night at supper.

Her children, Matt and Chloe, perked up with bright eyes and her husband, Mark, raised his eyebrows.

"What is it? What is it?" asked six-year-old Matt, jumping up and down in excitement as he and Chloe followed their mother over to a bag in the corner.

Chloe, the quiet one, said little, but her wide eyes told Janis she was just as excited and curious as Matt. Janis set the brown box on the table.

Matt tore through the heavy tape on the box and lifted the lid. The straw-like packing looked like a giant bird's nest.

"Careful," said Janis, helping her two children ferret out the contents.

Matt pulled out a camel figurine, and then a shepherd. He handed each piece to Chloe who reverently set them on the table. Then Matt burst out with excitement, "It's a manger scene!"

"Man-jer," said Chloe.

Janis explained, "I saw it today when I was Christmas shopping. There I was with my cart overflowing with Christmas presents, and I'm thinking to myself, *just stay focused. Pay for everything and get out.* But looking over at this manger I couldn't resist."

She looked at Mark. "Funny how your memory plays hide-and-seek. I had forgotten about the nativity set from my childhood. I spotted this one, and it looked so much like the one I remembered—not one of those sophisticated, bisque porcelain sets, but an old-fashioned kind, like I had when I was growing up. I just had to get it."

Then Janis glanced over at her daughter, Chloe, who seemed to cherish anything miniature, dolls in particular. Chloe had an impressive assortment of small babies given to her by friends and relatives. And here before her was a delightful grouping of animals, people, even a mother and a father! They had captivated her attention—especially the tiny baby.

After setting up the nativity on the end table in the living room, Chloe could not resist touching the figures. "No, Chloe. Those are not toys. They are for decoration." Janis caught herself on the word *decoration* and explained further. "The manger scene is to remind us of the Christmas story."

Even though the children had heard the Christmas story in church, Janis and her husband Mark shared the story with them again. As usual, Matt was full of questions. Chloe listened with her usual, wide-eyed wonder. When Mark approached the part where Mary and Joseph needed a place to stay but found no room in the inn, Chloe spoke up with concern on her face.

"They didn't have a place to sleep?"

"It worked out okay, Chloe," said Mark. "They ended up staying in the stable. Baby Jesus was born there, surrounded by all the animals. His bed was a manger, which held the hay for the cows and other animals."

Chloe nodded as if she understood.

That night as Janis and Mark prepared for bed, Janis walked past the manger scene.

"Oh no," she exclaimed.

"What's wrong?" asked Mark.

"Baby Jesus is missing. He must have fallen out of the manger," she said looking around the other figurines on the table.

"Maybe the kids bumped into it, and it fell out," said Mark.

They both dropped to the floor and searched but found nothing but a gooey sucker covered with dust bunnies.

"I don't understand," said Janis. "Where could it have gone?"

"Don't worry about it. It'll turn up." Mark laid a reassuring hand on her back. "Let's go check on the kids."

❧

Upon peeking into the first doorway—soft sounds of peaceful slumber filled the room. Chloe's pale face was surrounded by ringlets of curly, dark hair, which made her look like part child, part angel.

As Janis leaned over the pillow to give her daughter a kiss, she froze and motioned toward Mark. Her eyes shimmered with amusement. "You've got to see this." she whispered.

Chloe's small fist lay tightly closed on her pillow. Nestled snuggly inside was baby Jesus, wrapped in a tiny blanket, fast asleep.

THE HUMBUG HOLIDAYS AND THE LEAN-TO SNOWMAN

PATRICIA LORENZ

We depend upon the Lord alone to save us.

Only he can help us; he protects us like a shield.

PSALM 33:20 TLB

I was going through the motions—everything a good mom is supposed to do before Christmas. I lugged out the boxes of holiday decorations, baked my every-year-the-same-two-kinds of cookies, and even bought a real Christmas tree for a change.

I was going through the motions, but my heart was bogged down with a dull ache. I wasn't looking forward to Christmas one bit. My divorce had been finalized the past April, and my ex-husband was already remarried.

My oldest daughter, Jeanne, was in Yugoslavia for the year as a foreign exchange student and wouldn't be home for the holidays. This was the first time that all four of my children wouldn't be with me for Christmas. Plus the annual New Year's Eve get-together at my folks' house in Illinois had been canceled.

I was tired and grumpy. My job writing radio commercials at Milwaukee's biggest radio station became more hectic every day. Nearly every business in town wanted to advertise during the holiday season, and that meant longer and longer hours at work.

Then there was the real nemesis, holiday shopping, a chore I kept putting off. I was supposed to be planning and buying not only for my annual holiday party for the neighbors, but also for Andrew's eighth birthday on December 27 and Julia's seventeenth birthday on January 4. How would I get through it all when "bah humbug" was on the tip of my tongue?

During the night of December 15, a snowstorm ripped through Wisconsin, dumping twelve inches of snow. Although Milwaukee is usually prepared for the worst, this blizzard finished its onslaught just before rush hour traffic, bringing the interstate highways to a standstill. The next day all the schools and most businesses were closed. Even the radio station where I worked, eighteen miles from my home, urged early-morning risers to stay in bed because the roads were impassable.

After viewing the picture-postcard scene outdoors, I forgot my down-in-the-dumps attitude, grabbed Andrew, and said, "Come on, buddy, let's make a snowman!"

Andrew and I scooped up big handfuls of the wet, perfect-packing snow and built a base fit for a kingpin. Andrew rolled a ball of snow for the next level into such a huge mass that I had to get down on my hands and knees to shove it toward our mighty base.

When I hoisted Andrew's third boulder onto this Amazon snowperson, I felt like Wonder Woman pressing a hundred pounds. As our snowman reached a solid seven feet tall, I carefully placed Andrew's bowling-ball-sized snow head on top with the help of a stool.

"He needs a face, Mom." While I smoothed the snow and pounded arms and a waistline into our giant snowman, Andrew ran inside and returned with a silly beach hat with built-in sunglasses for eyes and a Superman cape that we plastered on the back of the giant.

Andrew and I stepped back to admire our noble snowman, straight and tall, ruler of the yard. When I took their picture, Andrew's head barely reached the snowman's middle.

It was warmer the next morning, and when I looked outside the kitchen window I noticed that Super Snowman seemed to lean forward a little. I hoped he wouldn't fall over before Andrew got home from school that day.

Late that afternoon when I returned home after a hectic, make-up-all-the-work-from-yesterday day at the radio station, I saw that our snowman hadn't fallen over, but leaned even farther forward at a very precarious forty-five-degree angle. His posture reminded me of the way I felt: tired, crabby, out-of-sorts, and with the weight of the world on my shoulders.

The next morning Super Snowman continued so far forward that it almost seemed a physical impossibility. I had to walk out into the yard to see him up close. *What on earth is holding him up?* I wondered, absolutely amazed.

The Superman cape, instead of being around his neck, now dangled freely in the wind as old Frosty's bent chest, shoulders, and head were almost parallel to the ground.

My own shoulders sagged beneath the weight of depression each time I remembered that Christmas was almost here. A letter from Jeanne arrived saying that since Christmas wasn't a national holiday in Yugoslavia, she'd have to go to school on December 25. I missed Jeanne's smile, her wacky sense of humor, and her contagious holiday spirit.

The fourth day after we built the snowman was Saturday the nineteenth, the day I'd promised to take Andrew to Chicago on the train.

Andrew loved the adventure of his first train and taxi rides, the trip to the top of the world's tallest building, the visit to the Shedd Aquarium, and the toy departments of every major store on State Street. But I was depressed by the fact that it rained all day, that the visibility at the top of the Sears Tower was zero, and that the all-day adventure left me totally exhausted.

Late that night, after the two-hour train ride back to Milwaukee, Andrew and I arrived home, only to be greeted by the snowman, who by this time, after a warmer day of drizzling rain, was now totally bent over from its base and perfectly parallel to the ground...yet still balanced six inches above the slushy snow.

That's me out there, I said to myself, *about to fall face down into a snowbank. But why didn't our snowman fall? Nothing, absolutely nothing, supported the weight of that seven-foot-tall giant.*

Just like there isn't anything or anybody supporting me during this awful holiday season, I blubbered mentally.

I wondered, *what had supported the snowman in such a precarious position? Was it God in His almighty power? A freak of nature? A combination of ice, wind, rain, and snow that had bonded to the mighty Super Snowman?* I had a feeling there was a lesson to be learned from watching his decline. The lesson came to me gradually during the next two weeks.

On Christmas Eve, at the children's insistence, we attended the family services at our parish church and dined on our traditional oyster stew afterwards. Then Andrew brought out the Bible for the yearly reading of the Christmas story before the children and I opened gifts.

Later we attended a midnight candle service with friends at their church, and finally a phone call from Jeanne in Yugoslavia brimmed with good news of an impromptu Christmas celebration planned by the mother of the family she was staying with.

The next day some friends offered to co-host my big neighborhood party which turned into a smashing success. On December 27, Andrew was delighted with his three-person birthday party. The next weekend my out-of-town family got together for a long New Year's Eve weekend at my house, filling our home with the madcap merriment of ten houseguests who all pitched in to help with everything. And when Julia simplified another dilemma by saying that all she wanted for her birthday was a watch and "lunch out with Mom," I smiled all day.

I learned that no matter how depressed, overwhelmed, saddened, lonely, or stressed out we become, there's always someone or something to help us find or recapture our own inner strength, just like there was for the falling-down, stoop-shouldered Super Snowman.

During his four-day lifespan, he showed me an amazing strength from within…a strength that came to me gradually, bit by bit, as each person in my life stepped up to boost my faith and my spirits to heavenly skies.

It was indeed a holiday season to cherish.

THE CHRISTMAS
I GREW UP

TERRENCE CONKLIN, AGE 13

Honor your father and mother, that you may have a long,

good life in the land the Lord your God will give you.

EXODUS 20:12 TLB

It was 4 A.M. on Christmas Eve. My father was lying in my parents' bedroom with his cardiothoracic leggings on, his heart pillow to his chest for when he coughed, and wrapped in four or five blankets to keep him warm. He was recovering after surgery from his recent heart attack.

My little brother was sleeping on the couch and waiting for Santa to come. He hoped to "catch him in the act" this year. This was hardly unusual for this particular night of the year, if you overlooked the fact that downstairs, two other creatures were stirring—my mother and I.

With my father laid up after his brush with death, my mother was left to handle Christmas all by herself. And at thirteen, I was hit with the hard truth about Santa Claus.

Everything seemed completely wrong and unfair. I watched my mother wrapping last-minute gifts, placing on the tags, and carrying them up the stairs in exhaustion—of course, tiptoeing past my sleeping brother.

This had not exactly been what I had in mind for my Christmas break. I was the usual selfish teenager, who had spent the last week doing nothing but trying to get out of holiday chores. After all, I was supposed to be on vacation!

As if all of that weren't bad enough, that night I was dragged to the holiday services at church. But as I watched my mother, face on, from my position in the youth group choir loft, something changed. I saw her in our familiar pew, sitting there without my father. She was struggling to keep my brother from wiggling. She closed her eyes in a deep prayer, and tears began to flow down her cheeks. And in that moment, as if for the first time ever, I heard the commandment: "Honor your father and your mother, so that you may live long in the land the Lord, your God, is giving you."

That night my mother and I stayed up into the wee hours of the morning, stuffing stockings, filling the empty space under the tree, and trying not to trigger the train set that now encircled the tree stand and wake my sleeping brother.

Seeing how much my mother put into Christmas with an out-of-work, desperately ill husband and two young children, made me begin to respect her. I rushed to do anything she asked and did not grumble in my cranky, "teenage" way.

I wanted to honor both of my parents, always, and I would try to teach my brother to do the same. Especially when "Mrs. Claus" needed help.

The Christmas lights shone on my mother's face as we placed the last gift under the tree. But that Christmas I received a greater gift: I had learned honor and obedience, and I hoped we would all live long in the Lord.

THE GIFT OF LOVE, THE GIFT OF LIFE

JANET LYNN MITCHELL

But when the fulness of the time was come, God sent forth his Son,

made of a woman, made under the law, to redeem them that were

under the law, that we might receive the adoption of sons.

GALATIANS 4:4-5

> YOU CAN GIVE WITHOUT LOVING, BUT YOU CANNOT LOVE WITHOUT GIVING.
>
> —*Amy Carmichael*

I stood in awe as her contractions progressed. Gently, I dried her forehead from the sweat of labor. One moment we laughed and the next I wiped her countless tears. We both knew that today our lives would forever change.

Within hours, her contractions intensified. The doctor finally arrived. Quickly we moved to the delivery room. The coldness of the room was warmed by the knowledge of the miracle that was about to take place. I sat by her side, brushing her hair away from her face as I did my best to coach her.

With one final push, the baby emerged. The doctor cut the cord separating mother and child. The room held silence, except for the first sounds of a healthy cry. For a moment, time seemed to stand still. I took a deep breath as the nurse carefully bundled this precious newborn and laid her in my arms—*my arms*. For the young woman who had just given birth had chosen *me* to become the mother of her child.

As I touched and cradled my new daughter for the first time, I glanced at her biological mother out of the corner of my eye. As I lifted my face our eyes met; they spoke volumes. I nodded to assure her of my profound gratitude. As I lifted my newborn daughter and brought her to the lips of her biological mother, I took a mental picture as I watched the final kiss good-bye. My voice quivered as I tried to find appropriate words to express the overwhelming appreciation filling my heart. She smiled back at me through streaming tears, and I could see her obvious struggles as I began to bond with my priceless gift.

Walking to the newborn nursery, thoughts played in slow motion across my mind. I pictured God beholding His infant Son. I imagined Him touching His Holy Child and cradling Him within His bosom. Perhaps tears had formed in God's eyes as He conceived the provision, the plan He had created for the redemption of my sins. I wondered if God, too, lifted baby Jesus to His lips, kissing His Son good-bye as He handed His Son to Mary. I cried, as I could not find words to express my thanks.

Before this day I had never really known such an act of love. It was courageous, unselfish love that motivated the gift of life my daughter received. It was joy unspeakable to be given a child, to become a family. The memories of this day will be treasured forever. For through this experience I, for the first time, began to understand how deeply God loved me.

This Christmas, I walked into my newborn's nursery with a new perspective. My heart could now see the true miracle of God's love, the birth of baby Jesus. I experienced the awesome reality that God had chosen me to receive His child also. I opened my heart and graciously accepted the eternal and tremendous gift of God's only Son.

This Christmas, may you also receive in your heart the gift of love that God so fully gives, the gift of the Christ Child.

THE GIFT OF TOGETHERNESS

NANCY B. GIBBS

Now to him who is able to do immeasurably more than

all we ask or imagine, according to his power that

is at work within us, to him be glory in the church and

in Christ Jesus throughout all generations, for ever and ever!

EPHESIANS 3:20-21 NIV

Christmas Eve, 1996, was sure to be a very sad day. My parents' house had been the gathering place for our entire family for many years. That Christmas, unfortunately, things would be very different. As a matter of fact, I was afraid that life would never be the same for our family again. Just that previous spring, we had been forced into placing my father in a nursing home for round-the-clock care. Parkinson's disease had invaded his body, and dementia was quickly taking over his mind.

"HOW DEAR TO THE HEART ARE THE SCENES OF MY CHILDHOOD, WHEN FOND RECOLLECTION PRESENTS THEM TO VIEW."

—*Samuel Woodworth*

Less than five months later, Daddy broke his hip. The doctors told us that Daddy would never walk again. They were right. They also concluded that he would not live longer than six to twelve months. I was an emotional wreck, and I knew I couldn't face Christmas Eve at my parents' house without him. It just wouldn't be the same.

I felt that we had no reason to celebrate this holiday season. I wanted to forget the decorations, the turkey, but mostly I wanted to ignore the family gathering. Christmas just wouldn't be Christmas that year. I didn't want to bother with it at all.

I had pondered the idea of taking Daddy home for the day, but it seemed like an impossible feat. He would have to be transported by ambulance. A hospital bed was a must with him in his condition. He would also need to be attended by a nurse. With all the expenses of his medical bills and nursing home payments, there was just not enough money left for anything extra.

One day, while I was driving to the long-term care facility where Daddy lived, I heard an announcement on the radio. That particular radio station would be granting twelve wishes for Christmas. The thought crossed my mind that my wish would just be too big and too expensive, but I could at least let them know my greatest Christmas wish. I composed a letter, stating my heartfelt request. "I want my daddy to spend Christmas at home one last time."

One week later, I received a phone call. "Your wish is coming true!" the caller exclaimed over the phone. I was ecstatic. Immediately, in my heart, Christmas came alive! Magic filled my soul. Daddy was going to be home on Christmas Eve, just as every other year. My mother pulled out the Christmas decorations and turned on the joyful carols. Christmas was on, and Daddy was going to be home! What a wonderful and exciting day it would be!

Unfortunately, four days before Christmas Eve, Daddy became very ill. We rushed him to the hospital, and our hopes diminished again. After a long weekend of taking care of him day and night, exhaustion overwhelmed me. But the day before Christmas Eve his health improved. We talked with the doctors about releasing him from the hospital so he could go home for the day. With the doctors' blessings, our Christmas plans were back on again. Somewhere, I found a burst of energy and stamina, even though I was extremely tired. I knew in my heart that we would all spend one more Christmas Eve together in my parents' house.

There were so many things to do. The medical supply company donating the bed brought it to the house. They placed it beside the Christmas tree in the living room. They left a huge fruit and candy basket with a get-well card attached. The ambulance service was lined up and the nurse assigned to my parents' home lined out her final plans to be there. The kindness these angels expressed and the joy I felt were indescribable.

On Christmas Eve morning, I eagerly met the ambulance at the nursing home. We couldn't have asked for a more beautiful day. I explained to Daddy that it was Christmas Eve and that he was going home to spend it with us. When the medical technologists brought Daddy through the front door, he began to cry. Our entire family spent a day filled with Christmas joy with him. We opened gifts, ate turkey sandwiches, giggled, and enjoyed a wonderful day together, just as we always had.

When the day ended and the stars began twinkling above, I could tell that Daddy was growing weary. As we boarded the ambulance for the trip back to the nursing home, it dawned on me that a miracle had surely occurred that day. As a result of a simple letter I had written and the kind response of many caring people, our holiday was filled with joy.

When we returned to the nursing home, I said a prayer with Daddy, thanking God for the blessings of that special day. I tucked Daddy's covers. In just a few seconds, he was fast asleep. I gave him a Christmas kiss on his cheek and walked outside into the brisk air. I glanced up toward Heaven and felt God's power stronger than I had ever experienced it before. A sense of comfort surrounded me. I prayed words of thanksgiving in the middle of a parking lot, while gazing at the moon and stars above. My wish really had come true.

Almost two thousand years earlier a magnificent miracle had occurred in a little town called Bethlehem. Another miracle had surely occurred that day in my own hometown.

That Christmas turned out to be Daddy's last trip to the place that he called his earthly home. This past Christmas, Daddy spent Christmas Eve in his Heavenly home, free of pain and suffering.

I'll always be grateful for the people who cared enough to help make Daddy's last trip home a possibility. That special day gave us all the hope and courage we needed to face the trying days ahead. These kind people gave us the greatest gift that could possibly have been given—the gift of togetherness— just one more time.

$\mathscr{G}$IFTS IN THE SNOW

JAY COOKINGHAM

Praise be to the Lord, the God of Israel,

because he has come and has redeemed his people.

LUKE 1:68 NIV

There they were, packages of various sizes wrapped in Christmas paper scattered all along the snowdrifts in my front yard. I looked out my window wondering how long they would last in the snow and when my father would let us retrieve them. I was only seven years old.

In a fit of rage over something unknown to us, he had tossed them, along with the tree, out the door early that Christmas morning. It would be three days before he cooled down enough to let us bring them inside and several more before we could open them. I don't even remember what I got that year, but I do remember the image of packages in the snow. For years that memory, along with other similar "holiday events," shaped my dread of Christmas. That was until God gave me a Christmas experience that would change me forever.

In my early twenties I traveled with a gospel rock band, and from time to time we would participate in other ministry opportunities besides concerts. On one of these occasions, several band members and I went to New York City to serve in one of the many soup kitchens in the city; this particular one was run by the Salvation Army.

We arrived very early in the morning; but the line to get a hot meal was already long, and many were eager to get inside the shelter. We met with the leaders who filled us in on how the day would go. The setup was simple. One group would first listen to a quick Christmas message in the small chapel and afterwards move to the cafeteria to eat. This process would repeat itself until people and/or food ran out.

To my surprise, I was asked to give the first message and was quickly shown the way to the chapel. As the various groups of people shuffled in from the cold air, I saw through the open door that it had begun to snow. The collection of old and young, men and women, slowly found seats. Many were still drunk or coming down from a night of intoxicated waste. Against the white purity of the fresh snow, their filthy, smelly clothes stood out in stark contrast.

What could I say to move the hearts of such people? As I waited for the chapel to fill, the Lord brought back the memory of the scattered presents in the snowbank outside my home. He quietly said to me, *These are My gifts. They too have been scattered and thrown away. Tell them I desire to bring them home.* My heart and eyes were opened with those words, and I began to feel the heart of the Father towards these *"lost gifts."*

I began to speak. Reading from the Scriptures, I told them of poor shepherds, pretty much the outcast of their day, being the first ones to hear about the Messiah's birth, and by angels no less! I related to them that this story was about God's great love, and no matter how far they had fallen, He wanted them underneath the blessing of another tree—the cross, which His Son Jesus was born to bear for them.

I finished my small sermon, prayed for them, and released them to the hot meal awaiting them. All but one left the room. A young man my age waited and asked to speak with me. He shared his story, of how his father had thrown him out on the streets just a few months before Christmas. The message of God's love had deeply moved him, making him realize how much he needed God in his life and how he needed to forgive his own father. As we talked and prayed, God began healing much inside of me as well—from now on, Christmas would be different for the both of us.

Every Christmas since then I have learned something new and surprising. The memories, the stories and traditions, all collectively add to the discovery process I go through each year. It wasn't always so, but God has faithfully shown me the right attitude to dive into at Christmastime.

As a father, I have the privilege to be the one leading the celebration in my home. That opportunity helps build memories, traditions (maybe even some silly ones, just for fun), and creates unity for the generations to come.

Yet, more than 2000 years ago, in a small Hebrew town, something more powerful than tradition rocked the world. Celebrating the birth of Christ does more than change the way I "do" Christmas, it transforms the way I am, the "who" I am.

Because of that God injection into mankind, all the stories, memories, and traditions have become richer in my life. That gift inspires me to lead and enjoy the festivities with the focus on a Savior who came to give life and give it more abundantly.

AN ANGEL'S FIRST CHRISTMAS

GLORIA CASSITY STARGEL

For God so loved the world, that he gave his only begotten Son, that

whosoever believeth in him should not perish, but have everlasting life.

JOHN 3:16

My tinsel-edged angel wings in place, I waited with the rest of the cast for the shift change of our live manger scene.

Area residents looked forward each Christmas to the live nativity scene staged by the young people and adults of our church. On the front lawn of our church—the scene was complete with real animals and swathed in floodlights—our nativity scene was a remarkable sight.

A sense of anticipation filled the educational-building-turned-dressing-room that evening. Volunteers made last-minute adjustments to the humble robes of shepherds, the gold-trimmed garments of wise men, the soft folds of Mary's gown....

Suddenly, the director's head appeared in the doorway, "Time to go!"

Out we scurried into a blustery, below-freezing December night. A gust of wind whipped my angel wings, and it seemed as if I might take to the skies like the Christmas angels of old. The only thing anchoring me to the ground was the heavy clothing under my white robe!

In total darkness, whispering only, we stumbled in the direction of the stable, a temporary structure of rough slabs. Pine boughs on either side represented trees.

One angel climbed up to sit on top of the stable. Around at the entrance, a shepherd pulled and pushed a reluctant donkey into the stall while the rest of us took our places.

All at once brilliant lights switched on. There we stood, transfixed in time, mirroring to the world a glorious scene— Christ's nativity.

The star of Bethlehem, suspended by wire high in the air, beamed its light down onto the manger scene. Our angel wings glistened as windblown tinsel sparkled in the light. The only sound now was the melodic strain of "Silent Night" emitting from the speaker system.

For thirty minutes we remained frozen in place, each of us locked in private thoughts. Then something extraordinary happened. The reality of the occasion we were representing flooded my awareness like an ocean wave.

I'm uncertain what prompted the awakening. Perhaps it was when Joseph reached over and gently calmed the restless donkey—or when Mary lovingly consoled the baby in the manger. Or was it the hushed crowd, the view of small children staring in wide-eyed wonder? Maybe it was the glimpse of cars as they pulled to the side of the roadway, sitting in reverent silence, and then quietly driving away.

Whatever caused it, our nativity scene came to life for me that night. Christ's birth no longer seemed a distant piece of history. It was as if we truly were in Bethlehem, as if Baby Jesus Himself were cooing in the manger. And there, right in front of my eyes, stood three wise men, bearing gifts for the Christ Child.

For the first time, I *saw* those gifts, and in my reverie pondered the meaning of Gold, Frankincense, and Myrrh.

Gold. Gold is for a king. Only God could have told them that the tiny baby in the obscure stall was a King! I stood, awed, in the presence of royalty.

Frankincense, a sweet perfume. The Old Testament tells us that frankincense was offered in worship to God, and to God alone. These wise men accepted Jesus—cradle and all—as the Son of God! My own heart bowed before Him.

Myrrh. Strange that they should being myrrh as a gift. Myrrh was one of the bitter spices used for burying the dead. It meant suffering. Even at His birth, the wise men were giving tribute to a Savior—One who was to be a sacrifice for the sin of mankind.

As I stood beneath the star, I was overwhelmed with the vastness of God's love—that He would send His only Son to rescue *me!*

Who but a loving Father would send our Savior in such a sweet, precious way, *a little Baby,* so we could know He came for *everyone*—even the helpless.

And that He would send Him to such lowly surroundings so that we could know He came for everyone—even the poorest.

I felt a sudden urge to break ranks, to turn to the people and proclaim like the angels of old, "Behold, I bring you good tidings of great joy!" I wanted to call out, "He's here! Jesus is truly here!"

Instead I silently prayed for those who watched us there in the night. *May the scene we're depicting come to life for them as it has for me. May it forever be etched on their memories and in their hearts.*

Again I gazed at the manger. *Sleep on, dear Holy Infant, sleep on. Sleep—in heavenly peace.*

The floodlights went out. But the effect in my heart from that night lingers still. For through the years my benediction echoes over and over in my heart. *Live on, dear Holy One, live on. Live on, dear Jesus—in me.*

JUST CLOWNING AROUND

NANCY B. GIBBS

Let us not become weary in doing good, for at the proper time

we will reap a harvest if we do not give up.

GALATIANS 6:9-10

When I was asked to lead the children's choir at our church, no one mentioned that there were additional responsibilities that came with the job. Since I loved children, I was excited about my new leadership position.

The new church year began each October, and the nominating committee announced the names of the workers for the coming year. I had the job of teaching music to eight children. My class consisted of preschool children from the age of two to five.

Although I didn't have a beautiful voice, I had a joyful heart. The chairman of the nominating committee assured me that was what counted the most. I thought, *Anybody can teach songs like "Jesus Loves Me."* The kids and I hit it off right away. They loved me, and I dearly loved them.

But, before I knew it, parents were asking about the upcoming Christmas program. "The what?" I exclaimed.

"The program that you will be leading," they responded. That was when I discovered that the leader of the preschooler's choir planned the annual children's Christmas play.

For several years, the children presented a traditional Christmas program. They were precious. They used brilliant expression while reciting their lines and sang like happy little birds. I was very proud of each one.

The following year, however, I decided to do things a little differently. I thought the congregation might be growing tired of the traditional program which the children had typically presented, and this year, there were significantly more children.

There were more than a dozen kids anxious to participate, ranging in age from two to twelve. I rushed to the Christian bookstore and shuffled through books filled with seasonal plays. Nothing seemed to fit our needs. Some of the plays, which required the correct number of characters, were not appropriate for all ages.

I'll just write a play myself, I decided. One night, I drafted a program to accommodate our group of youngsters. The setting would be a toy store. The name of the program would be "Toyland." Two of the kids played the parts of the storekeeper and a last-minute shopper. One of the older children would pose as the original Saint Nicholas. The remainder of the children would come dressed as toys. We could have as many toys as we had children.

We practiced diligently during the next few weeks. Many of the children were still not sure what costume that they would be wearing.

"As long as you dress as toys I'll be happy," I responded at the conclusion of the last practice. We had all worked very hard on the props and at the rehearsals. By the night of the program, I was a nervous wreck and prayed that the program would go as planned.

"I'm never doing this again! It's not worth the headaches," I told my husband, Roy, on the way to the church.

"Everything will be fine," he said with a reassuring smile. "Just wait and see."

When we arrived at the church, I saw bunnies hopping around, several dolls, a robot, and a jack-in-the-box. I was amazed at the creativity. Before long, I saw children dressed as crayons and also a few made up as clowns.

This is going to be a great play, I said to myself. *All the actors are adorable!*

Just before show time, the smallest clown ran to me. He was no more than three years old. Tugging at my sweater he whimpered, "I'm scared, Mrs. Nancy. What do I do again?"

"Just go up there and act like a clown," I replied.

His mother and father beamed with pride, as did all the parents. The sanctuary was filled, and there was standing room only. As the lights slowly dimmed the program began. While the shopper bought her last-minute Christmas gifts, the toys stood perfectly still.

As I directed the program from the front pew, the song "Toyland" could be heard, softly at first, and then more loudly with each new stanza. Once the music began the toys came alive. Jack jumped out of his box and the other toys yawned and woke up.

The littlest clown looked at me and wiped his eyes. I was afraid he was going to cry. I threw him a smile, and he smiled back. Following my directions he acted just like a clown, jumping up and down, giggling, and laughing. The audience laughed as I frantically tried to get his attention.

Before long, I gave up. The littlest clown had stolen the show. He sang loudly into the microphone and made silly clown faces. The audience was in stitches. I couldn't help but laugh myself. I had lost total control of the play and the littlest clown. He had simply followed my instructions and acted like a clown.

"This was the best play ever," the pastor announced through tears of laughter at the conclusion.

The children received a standing ovation, and the littlest clown proudly bowed. He grinned at his appreciative audience, never realizing that he was the actor who had made the show complete.

"Did you see me clowning around, Mrs. Nancy?" he asked enthusiastically after the show was over. He was very proud of himself.

"I can't wait for next year," I later told Roy.

"Oh, so you're going to lead the program again next year too?" Roy asked.

"I surely will. It was a blast." I proclaimed. I laughed once again as I thought about the adorable little boy while he played his part—"just clowning around."

$\mathscr{G}$REEN INK

LAURA L. SMITH

Therefore, as the elect of God, holy and beloved, put on tender

mercies, kindness, humility, meekness, longsuffering.

COLOSSIANS 3:12 NKJV

"THREE
THINGS IN
HUMAN
LIFE ARE
IMPORTANT:
THE FIRST IS
TO BE KIND.
THE SECOND
IS TO BE
KIND. THE
THIRD IS TO
BE KIND."

—*Henry James*

The rush of Christmas was again upon me. I was opening a stack of Christmas cards, glancing quickly at photos of friends' children while listening to my four-year-old daughter rehearse the *Little Drummer Boy* for her preschool Christmas program. My mind swirled with commitments, cookie recipes, and carols, and then it froze.

Staring at the letter in my hand, I couldn't breathe. My ears burned as if I had just come out of the December cold into a heated house.

In this envelope there was not a Christmas card. Instead, I held a letter signed by Helen's four children, letting me know of her unfortunate passing. Forty-seven years had passed since

Helen Tibbals walked into my mom's living room. I dropped to my kitchen floor, while tears flowed down my face for the loss of this angel. And then, I sensed a certain relief in knowing Helen was in Heaven where she had always belonged.

I thought back to a story my mom had shared with me so many times before. She was living with her Grandma Erskine in a small home with three brothers, a sister, and her mother.

She told of one specific day when a knock echoed at the front door where a slim, redheaded woman with her teenage boy stood smiling. She watched in awe as the two strangers carried armloads of packages, wrapped in red with their names written on white tags in green ink, into the house. They also brought a pine tree, strings of colored lights, and glass ornaments, transforming the drab room from black and white to Technicolor!

The woman in the green silk dress introduced herself as Helen Tibbals and her awkward looking son as Todd Junior. She was a member of First Community Church, the same church my mom's family attended, and explained that she had taken a paper gift tag, shaped like the star of Bethlehem, off the Christmas tree standing in the church vestibule. It had the family's name on it.

Helen was all lipstick and smiles and smelled like the department store downtown. The sharp scent of peppermint filled the room, as Helen opened a box of candy canes and invited the children to join in decorating the evergreen. All the while, she asked questions about the kids as if they were her own.

My mom had so many questions for her, but was too shy to ask them. *Where had this angel and her little helper come from, and why did she care so much about this family?*

Helen was the gift of Christmas present. A reminder that despite a father who had deserted them, a terminally-ill mother, and the fact that all five of the children lived in a two-bedroom home with their mother and grandmother, God's hope and love lived in the world.

My mom has told this tale so many times I can instantly smell the scent of spruce and hear the clang of ornaments in that living room at any given moment of the story.

Helen became much more than a Christmas gift; she became a part of our family. Until my mom and her siblings graduated from high school, Helen regularly brought them school supplies, new clothes, and chocolates. She even sent them to summer camp each year. When my grandmother struggled with breast cancer, Mom said Helen would bring candy bars and magazines to the small home as if she were Grandmother's sister. When my mom, aunt, and uncles were in college, Helen wrote them faithfully, always using her signature green pen. Helen attended my grandmother's funeral, my mother's graduation from high school, and my parents' wedding.

Helen's generosity expanded to the next generation as she adopted my brother and me as grandchildren, including us in her umbrella of selfless giving. She often invited us to her home each summer for a feast and a stroll around her goldfish pond. Every birthday, gifts would arrive at our house, our names written across the top in green felt-tip marker.

I remember the excitement of seeing an envelope with my name scrawled in Helen's green ink every Easter and Valentine's Day. Poinsettias in December would bear her green signature and even the place cards at the annual Christmas dinner at her club, where she made sure the waiter kept our Shirley Temples refilled, were written in green ink.

When my husband, Brett, came home from work he found me still weepy as I pulled a boiling pot of pasta off the stove, sat it in the sink, and scooped up our toddler, Matt, whose hands reached to the sky while saying, "Hold, Mama, hold!"

I pointed to where the tear-spotted letter lay limp on the counter.

Brett set his keys down and scanned the note. He turned and wrapped his strong arms around my quaking body. Soon I was able to exhale and push a smile onto my streaked face.

"Honey, can we get an extra name off the Giving Tree at church this year?" I swallowed hard, and then continued. "Helen came into my mom's life by picking her name from a tree. I would like to follow her example." A tear zigzagged down my cheek and then another.

"Of course," he smiled and kissed me on the tip of my nose.

The next day when Brett came home from work, he pulled two yellow pieces of paper cut in the shapes of mittens from the pocket of his parka.

"The directions said to put our name on the half of the tag still hanging on the tree, so the church would know who was responsible for that gift," Brett explained while easing his briefcase off his shoulder. "I guess that way, no child will go unaccounted for."

I nodded while drying my hands on the holly-embroidered towel by the kitchen sink.

"I wrote B. Smith on this tag, our tag," he said holding up one of the canary-colored cards.

I started to walk towards him.

"And on this mitten," my husband's turquoise eyes twinkled, "I wrote H. Tibbals—in green ink."

GIFTS FROM THE HEART

KAREN MAJORIS-GARRISON

You should remember the words of the Lord Jesus:

"It is more blessed to give than to receive."

ACTS 20:35 NLT

It had been the perfect winter night to view Christmas lights. "Hurry, kids!" I shouted upstairs to my children. "Daddy's already outside warming the van."

Within minutes I heard excited voices. "Mama! Mama!" my six-year-old daughter Abigail shouted, sliding on her behind down the carpeted stairs. "Is the hot chocolate ready?"

"It's in the van," I told her, smiling as my two-year-old son Simeon tugged at my shirt. We were all attired in our pajamas. After all, this was a Christmas tradition where we'd get into our sleepwear, pack a bag full of munchies, and head into our van looking at decorations on neighboring houses.

We had just stepped out of the door when Abigail surprised me by asking, "Mama, can you give me more money for doing my chores? I want to buy you, Daddy, and Simeon the best gifts for Christmas!"

"The best gifts are those that come from the heart," I grinned, recalling how she had drawn me a picture of a rainbow the day before, after learning I'd been feeling under the weather.

"You mean that instead of buying people things at the stores—that there's other ways to give them gifts?"

"Yep," I answered, securing her seat belt. "It goes right along with what we learned this morning at church."

She grinned, quoting Acts 20:35: "'It is more blessed to give than to receive.'"

I kissed the top of her head, and once we were all settled into the van, we opened the bag of goodies. The kids cheered aloud as we passed by numerous homes adorned with Christmas splendor.

It began snowing lightly when we rounded the familiar neighborhood that my husband Jeff and I had lived in years ago.

"You lived there?" Abigail asked, pointing to a newly renovated two-story house. "Why'd you move?"

I answered her many questions until Jeff turned the van onto Reeves Drive, and the headlights flashed onto the first brick home of the street. The house appeared disturbingly dark compared to the bright lights displayed by its neighbors.

"The people who live there must not like Christmas," Abigail noted from the back seat.

"Actually, honey," my husband said, stopping the van briefly along the curb, "they used to have the best decorated house in the neighborhood. An elderly couple lived there. Mommy and I used to visit them when we lived nearby." Jeff pointed to the reflective letters on the mailbox. "Looks like she still lives there."

He clasped my hand, and I sighed, remembering Lena and her husband and how they used to take such joy in decorating their home for Christmas. "It's for the children," they'd often say. "We like to imagine them in the back seat of their parents' cars. Their little faces full of Christmas magic as they look at our home."

"Why don't they decorate it anymore?" Abigail asked, bringing my attention back to the present.

"Well," I began, remembering the dark days when Lena's husband had been hospitalized. "Her husband died a few years ago, and Lena's very old. She only has one child, and he's a soldier living far away."

"Tell me what she's like," Abigail said, and for the next few minutes Jeff and I filled her in on the kind things Lena used to do. How she often baked homemade cookies and would invite us over after church.

"Can we visit her now?"

Simeon met Abigail's question with enthusiastic agreement, and I shared our children's excitement. Both Jeff and I looked down at our attire.

"I knew this would happen one day," he said, rubbing his forehead. "First I let you talk me into wearing pajamas in the van, and now you're going to want me to actually go visiting, right?"

☙

I kissed his cheek, and an hour later, after leaving Lena's home, Abigail and Simeon clutched the crocheted tree ornaments Lena had given them. "I wish I had a gift for her," Abigail said, waving at the elderly woman standing in her doorway.

The next morning, my children busied themselves upstairs on an unknown mission. After rummaging through drawers, closets, and toy chests, they descended the stairs wearing toy construction hats, snow boots, and Simeon's play tool belts.

"What is all this?" I laughed. "Are you going to fix things around here?"

"Nope," Abigail smiled brightly. "This is our gift to Lena. Since she's too old and doesn't have anyone to do it for her— WE'RE going to decorate her house for Christmas!"

Her words brought tears to my eyes. "That's a wonderful idea," I said, calling their father. "But I think you'll need Daddy and me to help. Is that okay?"

"Sure!" They replied.

Hours later, we stood with Lena on her sidewalk, looking at our handiwork. The lights we had found in her basement were shining with pride over snowcapped arches and windows. Candy canes lined the sidewalk and welcomed passersby to the Nativity scene that Abigail and Simeon had positioned on the snow-covered lawn.

A car cruising along slowed its speed to view the lights. Two children peeked from the back window, their faces full of excitement. Lena watched them, her eyes aglow.

It had been a day full of hard work, but it was worth every second to see the elation on her face. She disappeared inside her home and returned carrying a tray of freshly baked cookies.

Abigail reached her hand inside my coat pocket and clutched my fingers. "I feel what Jesus meant, Mama," she sighed, her dark eyes content.

"About what, sweetie?"

She leaned her head against my arm, and replied, "It is much better to give than to receive, especially when you give from your heart."

I kissed her cheek, so proud of her for using her own heart to think of this, and then I turned to my husband.

Our eyes met, and he smiled. "Looks like decorating Lena's house can be added to our list of Christmas traditions," he announced, and the kids heartily agreed.

THE FRUIT BASKET DELIVERY

NANCY B. GIBBS

But the fruit of the Spirit is love, joy, peace, patience, kindness,

goodness, faithfulness, gentleness and self-control.

GALATIANS 5:22-23 NIV

Christmas excitement was in the air. Our church youth were gathered in the church fellowship hall to prepare fruit baskets for homebound people in our area. While some of the kids were arranging baskets, others were addressing brightly decorated Christmas cards. Each child was anxious to share a portion of his or her joy with someone in need.

Each year, it was tradition to bundle up the children in warm coats, mittens, and hats. We would then take them caroling, delivering fruit baskets and the joy of Christmas into many lonely homes. It was obvious that our off-key carols and gifts were something these lonely and elderly people looked forward to each year.

Once we completed the rounds, we either took the kids out for pizza or went back to the fellowship hall to enjoy Christmas food, fun, and games. Like the people we visited, the kids looked forward to the annual event, as well.

On this particular year, we were about halfway through our list of homes to visit when the van pulled into a driveway. The kids all jumped out, singing gaily to themselves. I followed them to the front door of the humble home. At first I wondered if anyone was there, but then I heard the faint sound of the television. One of the children knocked. At the count of three everyone began singing, "We Wish You a Merry Christmas."

The door creaked as it opened. The lady of the house peeked out. She was shivering. While the children sang, she smiled. Her husband slowly made his way to the door. He had a shallow smile on his face.

"Come on in," the lady invited. One by one the kids filed inside, spreading their Christmas joy. The gentleman showed them to the living room. I heard stories that only a grandfatherly man could tell. Following each tale, I heard bursts of laughter. I stood in the kitchen with the lady.

"Would you sit down for a spell?" she asked.

"Well," I said and pointed toward the room where the kids were. I wanted to tell her how many more stops we had to make, but she didn't give me a chance. So I pulled out a chair and sat down across the table from her.

"We have had a rough week," she interrupted. "We found out last Monday that my husband has pneumonia. The doctor told him that he had to stay inside or he would get much sicker. The weather is so nasty these days." She paused for a few seconds, trying to regain her composure. "With my illness, I can't hang out clothes, and he really isn't able to, either. But he tried anyway this morning. I am so worried about him."

"Neither of you need to be hanging out clothes in this kind of weather," I followed. "It is entirely too cold outside."

"Our clothes dryer broke last week, and we don't have the money to have it repaired," she explained. "It's about twenty years old. It has probably seen better days."

My heart went out to her. I reached across the kitchen table and took her feeble hand. It was soft and warm. I imagined all the people whose lives she had likely touched with that gentle hand over the years. She had been a faithful church member until she was stricken a few years earlier with a terminal illness.

"Do you have plenty of food to eat?" I asked.

"We'll get by," she answered. I glanced around the kitchen but didn't see any food.

Maybe there's some food in the cabinets or the refrigerator, I reasoned.

Suddenly, I heard a calming song being sung by the children in the other room. I glanced at the lady's face. The vision I saw wasn't a calm or bright feeling. I saw lines of worry and fear. I wondered what I could do to help her.

Christmas should be a happy time, not a time filled with pain and worry, I thought.

The children passed out hugs and ran back to the van, where the other adults were waiting for us. The chaperones took turns getting out at each house to keep from being totally worn out after the fruit basket delivery was complete.

I crawled back into the van. "That's a sad situation," I announced.

"What do you mean?" one of the deacons asked.

I explained the circumstances. The children stopped talking and listened, as well. For a few minutes, silence engulfed the van. I am certain there were many tears being shed inside that dark van.

"I have an idea," one of the kids said. "Let's buy them a dryer."

"Great idea," an older youth agreed. "But where will we get the money?"

After we finished our fruit basket deliveries, we returned to the fellowship hall and put our heads together. We made a plan. The next day during the Sunday service, we would explain the circumstances to the church members and ask for a love offering. One of the deacons volunteered to pick up the dryer, deliver, and install it if we received enough money to purchase it.

"A dryer costs a lot of money, and we all have to participate to help the members fully understand the problem," I explained. "So we all need to be here tomorrow morning."

The next morning, the kids filed into the sanctuary. They began talking with the members sitting on the pews. An announcement was made about the need during the service. A love offering was taken at the conclusion of the service.

"There's no way this small crowd will be able to come up with enough money for a dryer," I whispered to my husband.

"With God all things are possible," he reminded me.

I saw money piled high in both offering plates. Since it looked like a lot of one-dollar bills, I didn't expect a large amount. But to my surprise, we had enough money for the dryer, the needed hookups, and we even had some extra money left over! We all cheered and shouted, realizing that our efforts had surely paid off.

The next day, a brand-new dryer was purchased by the deacon. He pulled onto the elderly couple's driveway. The lady peeked out and began to cry when he and another deacon started to unload it. In an hour or so, the dryer was hooked up and ready to go.

Remembering the card and the extra money collected, he announced, "Oh yea…I almost forgot, Here's some grocery money!" The couple embraced and thanked the deacons and God for the gesture of love and goodwill that was given to them that Christmas.

That sweet couple now resides in a place far from here. There is no need for a dryer in their mansion and no room for hunger or pain. But somewhere in my heart, I believe that couple still remembers the Christmas that a bunch of bundled up kids put their heads together and gave them something much more valuable than a basket of fruit—they shared an act of kindness, a renewed Christmas spirit, and a big chunk of their hearts.

OLIDAY MAKEOVER

SHAREN WATSON

And he hath put a new song in my mouth, even praise unto our God:

many shall see it, and fear, and shall trust in the LORD.

PSALM 40:3

"I don't want to go!" I yelled to my mom and promptly slammed the door.

Christmas break was just around the corner, and I was a senior in high school. I'd made plans, plans that didn't include a trip to my dad's house halfway across the country. I thought of all the dates I'd miss, all the Christmas parties, and hanging out with my friends. Typical teenager stuff.

My mom knocked quietly at my door. "Come in," I said. "Mom, why do I have to leave for the holidays? Don't you want me here with you?" *Maybe that will leave a little sting of guilt,* I thought.

"I know you're not happy with my decision to make you leave, but I'm doing this for you. You'll be graduating next year, and probably going off to college or working full time. You need to do this, Share. It may be one of the last times you spend the Christmas holidays with your dad." Mom's eyes searched for something inside of me, imploring me to see the importance of this visit. "This trip isn't up for debate. The tickets are already paid for. Your dad is expecting you. He'll meet you at the gate."

My posture spoke volumes admitting complete defeat. No words would change the situation now. I was as good as on the airplane. I refused to say anything to my mom, but knew she was right. I needed to make this trip to see my dad, even if I did resent it. I opened my suitcase and started packing my things.

Before I fell asleep, I prayed. *God, I really don't want to go to my dad's...you know that, and I feel so guilty about it. But it's so hard, Lord!*

I set my alarm for 6:15 A.M. to ensure that I'd have plenty of time to make my flight and fell into a fitful sleep.

"Sharen, Sharen." My mom shook my bed. "It's time to get up."

"Didn't my alarm go off? I didn't want to get up until 6:15." I whined.

"Yes, actually it went off three times, and its 6:30 now. I don't know how you hit the snooze button three times and don't remember." She rolled her eyes and smiled. "Teenagers." She said, exasperated and turned to walk away.

"Mom…" I called before she left my room. "I just want to tell you I'm sorry about last night."

"It's okay." She replied, her eyes glistening.

I jumped out of my bed and dressed quickly. Shoveling down a couple of pieces of toast, I prepared myself for the inevitable. I was getting on that airplane whether I liked it or not. And maybe it wasn't such a bad idea after all. I hadn't seen my dad since last summer, and I did miss him.

The airplane landed, and true to his word, my dad was waiting at the gate. "Dad!" I ran into his waiting arms.

"Sharen," he lifted me off the ground and whirled me around in the air, "I'm so glad you're here!"

"Me, too, Dad." I meant what I said, especially now that I was here exchanging hugs with my dad, stepmother, and little brothers. On the drive back to my dad's house, we stopped at The Old Spaghetti Factory in St. Louis, my favorite restaurant.

When we finally arrived at the house, my stepmother ushered me into the kitchen. "I made some divinity, and here's some fudge, Sharen. Do you want some?" my stepmother asked.

"Oh my gosh, I don't think so Marti. I'm stuffed, but thanks. I'll have some later. Speaking of candy though, do you think we can pull taffy tomorrow?" I loved making taffy with Marti. "We should do a green batch and a red one, okay?"

"Tomorrow it is, hon'. You want to help put up the decorations too?" she asked.

"Really, you haven't put them all up yet?"

"Not yet. I was waiting for another woman's decorating opinion." She chuckled.

I laughed. Marti was the only woman in a house full of men, and whenever I arrived for a visit, we did every girl activity you can think of, from hairdos to pedicures. We got along fabulously, and I called her my "Illinois Mom." The next day we got up early and pulled and packaged taffy. We were so sticky, but what fun we had!

"Sharen, how about you and I go shopping later?" Marti mumbled with a mouthful of the gooey treat. "You can show me what you want for Christmas this year."

"Okay. Sounds like fun." I mumbled in return. We both fell into each other's arms, laughing so hard we dropped to the kitchen floor.

"Hey, hey…ladies." My dad stood smiling over us. "What's going on here?"

"Oh nothing." I tried to say. The taffy was spilling over the sides of my mouth, and I was having trouble verbalizing anything clearly.

"I can see that." My dad smiled and winked at Marti. "I think I'll leave the two of you alone for a while. Maybe I'll be able to understand you better then." And with that he popped a piece of green taffy into his mouth and attempted to say something like "see you later." We just shrugged our shoulders and burst into laughter again.

"Okay…let's go!" Marti raced ahead of me out to the car, and I followed close behind. She turned the heater on as soon as she started the car, and about ten minutes later, we had finally thawed out.

"How about I take you to the beauty supply store?" Marti asked. "You can check out all the latest cosmetics, and we'll have a makeover while we're there."

"I'd love to do that! Thank you!" Marti was a beautician and makeup artist by trade.

As soon as we entered the store, I was mesmerized. There were so many lipsticks, blushes, eye shadows, and perfumes. We spent three hours of our afternoon there, applying facial masks, lotions, and nail polish. Marti brushed, dotted, smudged, and blotted beautiful colors onto my seventeen-year-old face.

"Do you like this look?" she asked, dabbing just a bit more finish powder on my forehead. Any doubts at all, and she scrubbed my face clean, starting all over again. "How about this?" she asked, as she taught me the tricks of how and where to apply the right colors.

I walked out of that store with a brand-new face (practically) along with a fresh new attitude. Our next stop was the mall. I needed to buy a few gifts for my family, and since it was Christmas Eve day, I needed to get it done quickly! I felt like a beauty queen walking through the stores that afternoon, a beauty queen with exhausted feet. Later, we headed home to wrap gifts and get ready for Christmas Eve.

The flames in the fireplace danced with glowing oranges, yellows, reds, and blues. The Christmas music played quietly in the background as my dad read the story of Jesus' birth from the Bible. I could barely take my eyes off the presents and noticed my little brothers sneaking closer to the tree.

"Hey, you guys! Get back over here." My dad grinned. As soon as he finished reading, he lifted his hands and said a prayer of thanks for Jesus' birth, death, and resurrection. He also prayed about the health and protection of our family and provision of food, shelter, and gifts. I peeked every once in a while to see if he was almost finished praying. He was known for lengthy prayers.

"Amen!" he finally said, and we all repeated after him. "Well, what are you waiting for? Open, open!"

I think I was the first one to the tree. I searched every gift trying to find boxes with my name on them. I handed my brothers their presents and continued rummaging through the rest. Satisfied that I had located every gift belonging to me, I looked at the small stack of boxes. Slowly, I took the first one and began to meticulously unwrap the paper, savoring the moment.

"Oh my gosh…it's the lipstick from the beauty supply. How did you…?" A mischievous smile lit up Marti's face. I opened each present, finding every bit of the makeup that I had sampled earlier, except the perfume. No matter, I knew that Santa would deliver it for Christmas morning. I watched my brothers unwrap a few toys, and each of them received watches. Surely they would have more to open in the morning too.

"I can't wait until Santa shows up tonight!" I announced. My dad and Marti looked at each other. "I think I'll go to bed now. I want to be up early."

"Me too!" my youngest brother stood to follow me.

"Me too!" repeated my other two brothers.

My dad stood slowly to his feet and quietly explained that there would be no more gifts in the morning; this was it.

"You're just kidding, I know you are." I laughed.

"Sharen, I'm not. I'm sorry," he replied.

I hung my head, disappointed, but also embarrassed and deeply ashamed. "No…I'm the one who's sorry."

"Come over here, Sharen. Let's talk a minute." I joined him on the couch. "I didn't want to tell you this, but I think I need to now. Remember when I told you I was on vacation this month? Well, that's not completely true. I don't have a job right now. There are no more gifts, because there is no more money. But Sharen, God will provide, and He did provide for the gifts we bought. I want you to know, I'm not worried, and I don't want you to be either."

"But Dad, how are you going to pay your car payment and your rent?" I inquired.

"I'm not worried about that right now, Sharen. We'll just pray." And we did.

After our prayer I looked at my dad through tears and gave him a hug. "Dad, please take all my presents back. I haven't taken them out of the packages yet. I want you to keep the money, okay?"

"Absolutely not!" Marti sat down next to us hugging me too. "Those presents are for you, and you're going to keep them. They look so pretty on you, too, Sharen. Don't even think about returning them. And by the way, I love these earrings you bought me, and I'm not taking them back. God always provides, and I'm not worried either."

"Now, if you ladies don't mind, I'm ready for hot cocoa. Marti, is it ready yet?" asked my dad.

"The milk is on the stove. I'll go get it ready. Sharen, you want to help?"

"Sure, I guess so." I replied, sullenly.

"None of that!" My dad jumped in front of me.

"Hey!" I said.

"Hay is for horses!" my dad retorted. He's been saying that to me as long as I can remember, and I giggled.

"I love you, Dad, and you, Marti. Merry Christmas."

"Merry Christmas yourself, young lady. Now go and get that cocoa!"

I ran to the kitchen with Marti close behind me.

That Christmas, I learned more about giving and how to receive graciously than I'd ever known before. I'll never forget the sacrifice my dad made to provide an airplane ticket so I could be with him or for the gifts he gave me. In a time of financial struggle, my dad unselfishly gave to his family, and I learned to offer my gifts back in return. Embracing my family and faith with new meaning, my holiday makeover extended far beyond my skin, hair, and nails, making over my very life.

THE DAY GOD LAUGHED

MARCIA LEE LAYCOCK

For there is born to you this day in the city

of David a Savior, who is Christ the Lord.

LUKE 2:11 NKJV

"See what you have to look forward to now?" the whisper in my ear came from a friend in the pew behind us, and it made my smile widen. It was December 10th, and we were on our first outing with our new baby. She was only a few days old, but we braved the frigid Yukon winter to attend a Christmas pageant at the small mission church.

I knew the service wouldn't be a grand production. The church was just a hall, tiny and dilapidated. The carols were sung a cappella, without a pianist to help keep us in tune. The pageant consisted of six or seven children dressed in bathrobes, their heads in kitchen-towel wraps. The backdrop was made of cardboard stars covered in foil.

But I was seeing everything attached to Christmas in a brand-new way. The foil stars seemed to glitter more brightly than a chandelier. The carols were beautifully harmonious as though sung by angels. And the children...ah, the children made the story live!

My heart was bursting with thankfulness. I had just been given the desire of my heart, a precious gift—a child of my own.

We had been told it wouldn't happen, and after five years without conceiving a child, my husband and I tried to resign ourselves to that reality. I took great effort to hide the deep sadness I found almost unbearable. No one knew how much I wanted a baby, but the clues were there. I was angry much of the time. Convinced God was punishing me, I wanted to resent Him. The bitterness poured into all aspects of my life.

Until the day God laughed.

It was on the road to Mayo, Yukon. I was going to visit a friend, determined not to think about God or religion or any of the baffling questions my husband kept bringing up. But no matter what I tried, my mind would not rest. The question of God's existence and what He had to do with me would not go away. In desperation, I pulled my vehicle into a lookout point over the Stewart River.

The beautiful river valley stretched out below, but I barely saw it. In turmoil, I challenged God to do something to prove He was there. Then I realized how foolish I was, talking to a God I didn't even believe existed. At that point something happened which I have never been able to describe adequately. I "heard" laughter, like a grandfather chuckling, and the words, *Yes, but I love you anyway.*

I felt I was going insane. The turmoil had finally pushed me over the edge and now I was hearing things! I hopped into the car, stomped on the gas pedal of my truck, turned the radio up as loud as it would go, and fled.

My visit with my friend turned out to be more discussion on spiritual things, but by the time I returned home I had determined not to pursue Christianity. Besides, I had something else on my mind. I had been suffering from a strange flu. On about the seventh day of this "flu," the realization I was in fact pregnant flooded over me like warm rain. With it came a revelation of truth.

This was the "something" I had challenged God to do. The child growing in my womb was His answer, the proof of His love. He gave me the desire of my heart. She was born November 30, 1982.

"See what you have to look forward to now?" Oh yes, I saw. I saw a future filled with the knowledge there is peace without measure, grace without limit, and love without conditions. I saw a future suddenly bright because I believed in the Christmas story. A tiny baby, whose sole purpose was to live and die for me and all others, was born in Bethlehem. I saw the reality that Christ is still intimately involved in our lives here on earth. Though the church may be just a hall, the music less than perfect, and the costumes homemade, the story is exquisite. The Christmas story is a true celebration of God's profound love for us all.

CHRISTMAS DELIVERY

STEFANIE MORRIS

The meek and lowly are fortunate! for the whole wide world belongs to them.

MATTHEW 5:5 TLB

As soon as I turned south, the houses became smaller, the paint more chipped and faded. I began to feel a little nervous. *I should have waited until someone could deliver these Christmas gifts with me,* I thought.

I knew this neighborhood had a high crime rate. 9200... 9426...9614…I was getting a little closer. I felt anxious, hoping that I had the right address. Each year, our youth group raised money to buy Christmas gifts for boys and girls whose parents were in prison. This year we were given the names of two twin boys. Their grandparents were raising them while their mom served time. As far as I knew, there was no dad.

9806.... This was it. I pulled up in front of a small house. There was no one in sight and no car in the driveway. *God,* I prayed, *I am delivering these gifts for You. I need You to protect me!*

"MEASURE WEALTH NOT BY THE THINGS YOU HAVE, BUT BY THE THINGS YOU HAVE FOR WHICH YOU WOULD NOT TAKE MONEY."

—*Author Unknown*

I carefully locked the car door before walking up to the house. To my surprise, a tall young man answered the door. I didn't hear any sounds of either children or grandparents.

"Hello, I'm looking for Jackie Brown..." I paused, but the young man didn't say a word.

"I have some Christmas gifts that his daughter, Tanya, asked me to buy for her children," I explained.

"Uh, sure," the young man replied, and said nothing more. I still had no way of knowing if I was at the right house. Then he cracked open the door and shouted: "Matthew, get out here." A second young man walked out. There was still no sign of the children or their grandparents.

God, I'm trusting You, I prayed silently.

I knew many people, including my grandmother, would think I was behaving foolishly. But I was showing the love of Christ to the needy for Christmas, and I was going to trust Him for my protection. As an act of faith, I deliberately turned my back on the young men and led them to the trunk of my car.

The cynical part of me whispered that there might not be a Jackie Brown at this house, and that these young men might be leading me on just to get free Christmas gifts. Still, I began to hand the gifts over to them.

As I handed Matthew the last present, a football, I said a prayer in my heart; *Lord, let these gifts be the right ones that will bring joy to their Christmas.*

Proud of my feeble faith, I refused to think one nervous thought as I followed the men into the dark and silent house. Almost immediately I saw an elderly gentleman seated in a faded chair. *Thank You, Jesus!* I prayed silently.

"Mr. Jackie Brown?" I asked. He nodded. His face was lean and lined, a visible reminder to the passage of many years. "I'm Stefanie Morris."

"Tanya asked us to buy gifts for her children," I explained. "She also wanted us to tell them that she loves them very much." As I delivered Tanya's message, I looked over at the eight-year-old twins.

They were playing near a Christmas tree and looked happy and healthy. But there were no presents under the tree, and the house was sparsely furnished. It felt good to help a family that was clearly in need.

"Praise the Lord! He always provides," Jackie Brown said, looking at the gifts the young men carried. I took a seat while they placed the gifts under the tree. The twins immediately began poking, prodding, and weighing the wrapped gifts excitedly. Suddenly one boy gave a joyful shout, "It's a football!"

Yes, the Lord always provides, I agreed silently.

"I grew up in the depression," Mr. Brown explained. "Life was hard. There were ten of us. We were poor, but we didn't know it. We were in the country, so we farmed and hunted. We never had much, but we always had enough. The good Lord may appear to be slow, but He is never late."

I was moved. Life had been hard for Jackie Brown. He was probably in his late 60s or early 70s. He was not in the physical or financial position to take care of these children, but they needed him, and so he relied on God.

Jackie repeated the phrase that seemed to be the motto of his life: "Yes, the good Lord is never late." Then he asked me the very question I had been hoping to ask him, "Do you know the Lord?"

I felt humbled and close to tears. I had come to this house determined to show the love of Christ. Instead, I found a little home already full of His self-sacrificial love. I had been proud of my fragile, trembling faith that took me through their door. Inside, I found a frail man with a stronger faith than I had ever known. He had learned to trust God for his daily bread through decades of hardship.

I came to bring Christmas joy. Yet, Christmas was already there. The baby Jesus was born to just such a home as this.

"Praise God," I replied. "Yes, Jackie, I have seen the Lord!"

$\mathscr{W}$ISE DUDES

DARLA SATTERFIELD DAVIS

After Jesus was born in Bethlehem in Judea, during the time of

King Herod, Magi from the east came to Jerusalem and asked,

"Where is the one who has been born king of the Jews?

We saw his star in the east and have come to worship him."

MATTHEW 2:1-2 NIV

I had opened "The Christian Fine Arts Center" almost a year before when Christmas seemed to sneak up on me. We are a family-oriented establishment with a big emphasis on the teens in our area. We had been giving lessons in art, music, and sign language, as well as holding concerts every weekend for seven months. The time had just flown by, and the Christmas Parade was less than a week away from rounding our corner.

With the desire to reach the teens nearest to my heart, I had to laugh as all my artistic desires to *WOW the public* with our fabulous Christmas display melted and ran down the curb of

CELEBRATING FAITH AND FAMILY

pretentiousness. I had always dreamed of putting beautiful and breath-taking displays in the giant window of the old storefront that housed CFAC. But it was not to be. As is often the case, God had a different idea.

I was on my way home when I stopped at a light in town and glanced over at some young people putting up a nativity scene on the corner by their church. I saw three teenage boys with baggy pants, leather jackets, and knit caps pulled over their eyebrows. Each had their hands shoved deep down in their pockets, and were slouching as they stared down into the manger. The light changed, and I drove away with the image burned into my brain.

The next day we placed a homemade dummy in the window of CFAC. He was wearing a leather jacket, baggy pants, and a knit cap pulled down to his sunglasses. The dummy knelt on one knee and leaned on an electric guitar propped beside him. There was a giant cross on a hill in front of him with light shining down from the corner. *Wise Dudes Still Seek Him* was written on a piece of torn cardboard and placed beside him with debris and pop cans scattered around him on the floor. A colored disco light flashed and called attention to the scene.

It was a far cry from the elegant, exciting display I had dreamed of putting up in the downtown area, but somehow I knew it was right. Sure enough, cars began to slow as they passed by, then they began to stop and roll down their windows to look at the unusual display, and read the sign.

The kids standing outside during intermission on Saturday night had a lot to say about the display, as well. Some thought it was "cool," others "slammin'," and some didn't like it at all. I happened to overhear one such conversation as I made my security check, and had to laugh to myself. "Well, I don't like it," huffed a teenage girl. "It ain't even Christmassy or nothing. Look at all that junk on the floor. What's THAT about anyway!" she said flipping her hair and rolling her eyes.

The least likely looking Bible scholar I had ever seen stepped up to the question.

"Oh yeah, right, Christmas ain't got nothin' to do with Jesus and the cross does it?" he challenged.

"They should put the cross up for EASTER and a manger or something up for CHRISTMAS...duh!" she returned.

"Look," the street scholar retorted, "Jesus was all about the cross. Even when He was first born He was all about the cross. Whadda ya think He came for in the first place? Yeah, He got born, but that ain't it. He got born so He could hit that cross and save our sorry backs. They're just tryin' ta remind us that it ain't over, that's all." He knuckled the window for emphasis.

"He came, He died, He rose...yeah. But now what? That was a long time ago. The whole deal is today we're supposed to be seekin' Him, dressed like we are, doin' the stuff we do, but still looking for Him, man. And waitin' for Him to come back." He finished with a defiant jerk of his chin in her direction. Several others joined in the conversation and added their remarks, as well.

Like the display or not, the Christmas window had more than served its purpose in that one conversation. Jesus was born, died, and rose from the dead—now what? It is a great question to put out there, isn't it? Just look at all the different people who are seeking Him and telling His story *in their own words*. Generation after generation the message of Jesus Christ must continue. We must be "Wise Dudes," and keep seeking Him, and learn how to reach others so they can too.

THE CHRISTMAS WREATH RAID

NANCY B. GIBBS

For I long to visit you so I can share a spiritual blessing

with you that will help you grow strong in the Lord.

ROMANS 1:11 NLT

"SELFISHNESS MAKES CHRISTMAS A BURDEN; LOVE MAKES IT A DELIGHT."

—*Author Unknown*

While Christmas shopping one day, I discovered a clearance table of beautiful golden ornaments in a jewelry store. I picked out a few of my favorites, took them home, and admired the beauty they had to offer. I decided that they were much too pretty to get lost on a Christmas tree. Each one had many beautiful etchings and designs. The details made them gorgeous. I decided to use them to decorate 8-inch wreaths.

While admiring my decorated wreaths, I decided to make wreaths for my family members and friends, as well. I returned to the jewelry store. I found that the ornaments had been reduced even further. This time, I bought dozens of them. I thought of the many people who would enjoy having one in their home for the holidays.

Armed with a glue gun and ribbons of every conceivable color, I began making holiday wreaths. I spread them out all across my living and dining rooms. For several days, our family walked around the wreaths, dodged them while eating, and slept among them.

While I tied bows and glued ornaments, I reminisced about past Christmas seasons, and how special each one had been. I also thought about other people who had not been so fortunate. Some people in our community didn't have any Christmas decorations or a family with which to share the joy of Christmas. These people would be on the top of my list to receive a little wreath. I returned to the jewelry store and bought even more ornaments.

Upon completion, my husband, Roy, and I set out to make our "Christmas Wreath Raid." We visited many elderly people who lived alone. They loved our visits and hung the little wreaths, the only signs of Christmas, in their homes. It amazed us to see how much love a little wreath could bring.

After several days of delivering wreaths, I realized that I had made, and delivered with Roy's help, nearly two hundred tiny wreaths that Christmas season. They were decorated with love and filled many homes and hearts with the joy of Christmas.

We were actually the ones who received the greatest blessing that season as a result of the gifts we gave. It is God's way to share not only the gifts we can give, but also the joy and happiness of Christmas with those who are less fortunate.

Several years later, I once again visited the home of a sweet widow lady's home during the Christmas season. My heart was warmed when I saw that tiny wreath Roy and I had delivered to her a few years earlier. Hanging on her wall—it was the only sign of Christmas in her home.

ANGEL IN THE SNOWSTORM

THERESE MARSZALEK

For He shall give His angels charge over you, to keep you in all your ways.

PSALM 91:11 NKJV

Leaving the office parking lot at the end of the day in Minneapolis, I joined multitudes of snow-covered cars inching their way through an unpredicted blizzard. Although strangers, we all shared a common goal of reaching the safety and warmth of our own homes. It was by far the worst snowstorm I had witnessed in twenty years. Realizing I was likely going to be late picking up my young son, James, I silently prayed for grace with his baby-sitter.

The wheels of my little red Chevy spun as I pulled onto the freeway, entering an endless line of snow-covered cars. I grumbled when I noticed the red "check engine" light flashing its irritating eye at me. My frustration rose as I recalled having my company car serviced just the week before, yet the stubborn "check engine" light continued to flash intermittently.

While I concentrated on keeping sight of the car ahead of me, an obnoxious sound erupted from under the hood, threatening an already challenging trip home. I regretted a decision I made earlier in the week to delay scheduling an appointment for the car to be rechecked. My demanding schedule could not afford to squeeze in one more distraction.

The irritating noise from under the hood demanded increasing attention and made me question if my car would survive the homeward journey at all. I was thankful the windows of other cars were closed; I knew the undeniable grinding noise would attract embarrassing stares. Although the quickly mounting engine trouble cried for immediate attention, finding my way to a service station in the midst of this ferocious storm was not an option.

The blizzard raged fiercely, making it impossible to clearly make out the cars in front or behind me. To pull off the road would mean putting myself in danger's way. After all, *who would possibly offer help at a time like this?* Anyone on the road during this storm was focused on his or her own survival.

Crossing the main freeway, almost halfway to my coveted destination, a loud explosion sounded from under the hood.

Cranking the steering wheel hard to the right, I realized the power steering was gone. With only enough power to inch over to the side of the freeway, my wounded car crawled out of harm's way.

Then there was silence. The obnoxious grinding noise now gone, I heard only the howling wind sweeping across the freeway.

What am I going to do now, Lord? I fretted, feeling my heart race in my chest. *I can't get out of the car in this storm. I'm late to pick up James, and I can't even let his baby-sitter know I'm broken down.* Feeling overwhelmingly helpless, I closed my eyes and sighed, *Help me, Lord.*

Slowly opening my teary eyes, I peered into the foggy rearview mirror and noticed a small red speck in the distance out the back window. Watching the red form increase in size I realized a person was running along the freeway in my direction. *How can this be?* I thought. *Where did that person come from?*

As she neared the car, I rolled down the window to find a pleasant young woman in a fluffy red coat standing at my side. Her warm expression indicated no concern about standing on a crowded freeway in the midst of a monstrous storm.

"What can I do to help you?" Her welcome smile instantly calmed my racing heart.

After filling her in on my suspicious diagnosis of a blown engine, she offered to give me a lift to a service station and phone.

The brave stranger instructed me to wait in the car, then her red form disappeared once again into the raging storm. Minutes later, her royal blue car pulled over in front of me as she motioned me to get in. Feeling emotionally numb, I willingly hopped in the front seat, kicking the snow off my heels.

Anxious thoughts whirled through my mind as we drove to the service station. Being lost in thoughts of my pending dilemma, I didn't notice the peace and silence saturating the atmosphere in the car.

Without any instruction from me, my driver took the next exit and found the nearest service station. Surely, I thought to myself, she must be from around here.

As she pulled up to the door, I quickly exited the car, already focused on the next task at hand. Almost forgetting to thank my Good Samaritan for her kindness, I spun around before opening the service station door. The car was nowhere to be seen.

Speechless, I wondered how my rescuer could have disappeared so quickly. I searched every direction yet saw only blowing snow and cars spinning their wheels. My kind rescuer had vanished.

Who was that kind woman? I thought. Straining my eyes and looking in every direction once again, I suspected I may have been dreaming, but the biting wind and icy snow hitting my face reminded me this was surely not a dream.

After making arrangements to tow my wounded car, a kind service station worker drove me to my son's baby-sitter and then to our front door. With a sigh of relief, I welcomed the safety and comfort of my warm home.

Sinking into an easy chair with a steaming cup of coffee, I quietly pondered my journey through the snowstorm. *Who was the nameless woman who appeared as quickly as she had disappeared? Who was the kind servant who radiated such peace? Who was the mysterious rescuer who was willing to make such a sacrifice for me, a perfect stranger?*

Tears welled in my eyes as God brought to my remembrance that in the midst of my helpless trial, I had called out to Him for help. Filled with gratitude, I realized that my angel in the snowstorm was one sent by God. Once again, God poured out His everlasting grace and mercy. Once again, God was faithful.

Without even knowing it, I had been in the midst of God's special messenger sent in my time of need.

$\mathscr{T}$HE SURPRISE GIFTS

EVA JULIUSON

The generous soul will be made rich, and

he who waters will also be watered himself.

PROVERBS 11:25 NKJV

Walking out of my husband's hospital room, I was more despondent than ever. Struggling to balance the infant carrier that held our three-month-old baby and all the paraphernalia that goes everywhere with a new infant, I paused to shift my load and grabbed the hand of my five-year-old son, Ryan.

He was always quiet. He had learned to be silent, in order to be around his dad who had been deathly ill for the past three years. Ryan's young eyes had seen more suffering than most people do their entire lives. But the worst yet was this last month while his dad had been in the hospital.

As we made our way past the nursing station, my eyes caught sight of the brightly colored Christmas decorations. *Oh, my gosh! It was only a few days until Christmas!* It certainly didn't seem like it. *How could I ever help my husband or my children to feel any Christmas spirit?* Christmas had typically been a huge celebration for our family.

As we rode the elevator down, carefree memories of past holiday fun rolled around in my head. With my husband's long-term illness, how could I possibly help him or our four children experience Christmas? We had absolutely no money. Without insurance, Steve's medical bills and prescriptions had left us with overwhelming financial problems. Worst of all was the emotional wear and tear. How could we celebrate when everything seemed so hopeless? Walking to the car, the thought suddenly entered my mind, *Give gifts to a family who doesn't have any! Of course!*

Each Christmas since we had been married, we purchased presents for a family who didn't have enough money to buy gifts. Every year, that was what had really put us into the Christmas spirit. *That's what we'd do!* We didn't have any money, but I knew we could come up with something from home.

My excitement began to grow. By the time I was home, I remembered a girlfriend telling me about a young family living nearby who didn't have anything for Christmas, and I decided that's who we would surprise.

When I told my two older kids, they were as excited as I was. The search started all through the house for anything that would make a good gift. I found a full bottle of perfume and a bracelet that would be perfect for the mother. Eric, my oldest son, found a really cool car and a game for the little boy. My daughter, Chrissy, came out of her room with some stuffed animals, a doll, and a glittery little purse for the girl. Ryan had some clothes that were like brand new that were just the right size for the boy. And, in the closet, we discovered a whole box of wrapping paper left over from the previous year.

Our house was soon filled with giggles as we all wrapped the packages together. The kids made cards to attach to each gift that said, "From: Guess who!" Eric found a big box to put all the gifts in. Someone had brought us a basket full of fruit and nuts, so we added a few of these items to the box as well.

As I put the baby in the car, the kids worked as a team to load the box of goodies into the back. When we got to the apartment, we checked carefully to make certain that no one was watching. The kids grabbed the box and quickly put it in front of the door. Chrissy rang the doorbell, and then they all ran as fast as their legs would carry them back to the "get-away car" where I waited. As soon as the doors on the car shut, I sped away! All we could see as we drove away was the door of the apartment starting to open.

We had done it! No one had seen us! There was more laughter and sheer joy in that car than there had been in a long time. Each of the kids breathlessly reported about how they almost got caught and wished they could see their faces when they opened the gifts. I told the kids that this is what Christmas is all about. God wants us to give something of ourselves to someone who needs it. We all felt so good to be able to share with someone else who was having a hard time. It was our Christmas gift to God.

Our faces were still glowing with smiles when we got home. I stopped to check the mailbox. The mail hadn't come yet, but there were six envelopes inside. Each one was addressed to a separate member of our family. I curiously opened mine and discovered a $100 gift certificate for clothes.

Each of the children found the same gift in their envelope! I could not believe it! My heart was completely overwhelmed, and I couldn't wait to tell my husband.

We tried to give something of ourselves for God, and He gave us even more! You just can't outgive God!

$\mathcal{G}$OD'S PRESENCE

TONYA RUIZ

In Your presence is fullness of joy.

PSALM 16:11 NKJV

I turned on the light and reached for the ringing phone on my nightstand.

"Hello?"

"Tonya, it's Mom. Sorry to wake you up so early, Honey, but I wanted to let you know that Grandpa died."

I pulled my huge pregnant body out of my warm bed, waddled into the living room, and plugged in the lights on the Christmas tree. As I looked at the brightly wrapped presents, my eyes filled with tears. I wondered how I would tell my three little children that their precious Papa died on Christmas Eve. Poor Papa, he had been blind for years, but he loved rocking my Zachary and listening to Ashley and Lindsay sing.

After breakfast, I told the kids, "Last night Papa moved to Heaven." It was hard for any of us to be joyful. My six-year-old busy-bee, Ashley, tried to take her mind off her loss by making her bed and cleaning up her room. My five-year-old, Lindsay, snuggled close to me, holding onto her blankie and sobbing, "I already miss my papa."

"Presents, Mommy, presents," Zachary said gleefully while shaking a gift.

"Stop playing with those gifts!" I scolded him for the zillionth time. Then I foolishly tried to reason with a two-year-old. "Sweetie, I know you're excited and it's hard to be patient, and you've been waiting for a long time. But you can't shake the presents or rip the paper off of them, yet." Zachary crinkled up his nose, smiled, and then began taking the candy cane ornaments off the tree and putting them into a pile. *I give up,* I thought, *I'm already exhausted, and it's only eight o'clock in the morning.*

Later that day, at my parents' house I asked, "Do you think we should cancel our Christmas party?"

My mom had already decided, "Papa wouldn't want the kids to miss out, so let's just do what we'd planned."

That evening, my brother, sister, nieces, and nephews, came to my parents' house. The adults tried to put on happy faces, while the children were joyfully decorating the lopsided gingerbread house with frosting and candies. Finally, it was time for opening gifts. My girls immediately tried on their new dress-up clothes, and Zachary's chubby little hands unwrapped toys, toys, and more toys.

The next morning, with logs burning in our fireplace, my husband Ron read the Christmas story from the gospel of Matthew. Then we let the children open their brightly wrapped presents and eat candy from their stockings. That afternoon, for the grand finale, we bundled the kids in their jackets and drove to visit my husband's brother. Zachary was ecstatic when he realized there were even more colorfully wrapped gifts waiting underneath their tree.

Sadly, the following day, we all attended my grandfather's funeral which was held in a little white chapel. Holding onto my husband's arm, I waddled in with my little ones following like ducklings. We filed into the wooden pew, and little Zachary was sitting by my side. As the organist finished playing "Amazing Grace," I opened my purse and began searching for a tissue.

The gray-haired pastor stood up behind the pulpit and began to pray, "Lord, we thank You for Your presence here today...."

At which point, Zachary jumped up on the pew, stretched out his arms, and with a smile from ear to ear, yelled, "Presents, yippee! More presents!"

Everyone laughed and turned to see the noisy culprit, whom I was gently wrestling onto my lap. The pastor looked over at me, winked, and said, "Actually, the little guy has a point. I wish everyone was that excited about God's presence. Maybe we've all learned a good lesson today. God's presence really is a present."

I leaned down and kissed Zachary's little cheek and whispered, "I love you" into his ear. He nuzzled his face into my neck and fell asleep looking quite angelic.

ALL IN THE HEART

LISA ERLER

The people walking in darkness have seen a great light; on those

living in the land of the shadow of death a light has dawned...

For to us a child is born, to us a son is given, and the government

will be on his shoulders. And he will be called Wonderful Counselor,

Mighty God, Everlasting Father, Prince of Peace.

Isaiah 9:2,6 niv

"IT IS
CHRISTMAS
IN THE
HEART
THAT PUTS
CHRISTMAS
IN THE AIR."
—*W.T. Ellis*

Christmas music hummed from the stereo while I finished preparing Christmas dinner for my husband, Matthew, and our three young children. The ham, glazed with brown sugar and molasses, cheesy hash brown potatoes, and green bean casserole sputtered in the oven. Only the blueberry pie beckoned.

As I mixed the ingredients for the crust, my three-year-old daughter climbed onto the counter. "Can I help, Mommy?" she asked in her Mickey Mouse voice. Mixing one-half of a cup of ice water into two cups of flour mixed with a bit of Crisco takes a certain knack. How much help could tiny fingers offer?

I looked up from my task into her chocolate eyes and happy smile, and I simply could not crush her heart by saying no. I finished mixing the crust and formed balls. "Can I help?" Rachael asked again. What could I let her do? I pulled out the wax paper and rolling pin from the cupboard. Setting the ball of dough in between two pieces of wax paper, I struggled with the paper slipping over the counter while I rolled.

"Can I help?" Rachael asked again.

I looked up into her eager eyes and nodded. "Hold this paper for me so I can roll out the crust."

Rachael giggled and said, "Okay, Mommy."

With her hands holding down the wax paper, I was able to finish rolling out the crust. Rachael jabbered away as I placed the crust into the pie plate and dug the blueberry pie filling from the counter. "Can I do that?" Rachael asked as I began spooning the filling onto the crust. I finished with the first can and opened the second one for her to do. As she dumped the filling into the pie plate, some dropped onto her knee. "Oh, no," she said. "I'm sorry." I looked down at her dirty knee and countertop and said, "It's okay, Sweetie." I helped her finish putting in the rest of the blueberries.

While I was cleaning off her pants and the counter, I recognized the words to another Christmas song playing in the background, and began to sing along, "Christmas is all in the heart…"

Still, my heart felt heavy. *How can Christmas be in the heart, when my extended family of brothers and sisters were spread out over the Midwest and no longer came together to celebrate the holidays?* The memory of singing Christmas carols with my sister to my dying father was still strong in my mind. I choked up; never again on this earth would I sing to him. *How can Christmas be in a grieving heart?*

Still, the song played on. At that moment, the baby in my tummy kicked.

I paused.

I looked at the pie that still needed its top crust and to my sweet girl watching me with adoring eyes from the counter; she wore her new princess pajamas. My eyes scanned past the messy kitchen, past my railings trimmed with evergreen garland and Winnie-the-Pooh lights, to the red and gold Christmas tree in my living room where we had opened presents that morning.

Suddenly, the angst of a moment earlier dissolved.

Christmas began in God's heart when He gave the most perfect gift of all—His Son. Christmas would always be in a heart willing to worship that little baby boy named Jesus. The trimmings of Christmas often shine brighter than the humble manger, but it is the manger's gift that must glow in our hearts.

The pie needed to be finished. Little Rachael needed clean pants. Christmas dinner needed to be set on the table for our little family to enjoy.

This time, as I finished the preparations, my heart felt lighter. I thought of the Christmas seasons to come when my daughter Rachael and this new daughter soon to be born would be helping me bake another blueberry pie (or maybe cherry) for Christmas dinner.

CHRISTMAS BUNDLE

BARBARA MARSHAK

What he desires, that he does. For he will complete what

he appoints for me; and many such things are in his mind.

JOB 23:13-14 RSV

Like many families, everyone was coming to Grandma and Grandpa's for Christmas Eve, and Mom busily fussed in our narrow kitchen with last-minute dinner preparations. A bright, red Christmas apron hugged her plump figure, her short, gray curls pinned in place. In her calming nature, she instructed my fourteen-year-old sister to make room on the small table for the big, blue roaster filled to the rim with a potato hot dish.

Half dozing, my father was in the recliner, his thick, salt-and-pepper hair combed back in the same stylish wave he'd worn since his teens, relishing the quiet while it lasted.

Unlike many families, however, I claimed the title of aunt before I was even born, and at the young age of seven I already had thirteen nieces and nephews. With five of my six older siblings married or living on their own, it was a rare treat to have them all home on Christmas Eve.

"They're here!" I exclaimed, my nose pressed against the cold window. Jumping down from my position on the back of the couch, I raced to open the front door, the fresh snow sparkling under the December moon. Once again I had insisted on wearing my flower girl dress from my older sister's wedding. I loved the fancy lace and ribbons, wanting to feel special for Christmas.

"Merry Christmas, Grandpa," they chimed, coming through the front door one by one.

"Merry Christmas," he replied in his gentle manner.

Suddenly laughter, chatter, and footsteps filled the house as everyone handed over coats and presents. Secretly I cherished the chaotic atmosphere whenever they all descended, wishing they could stay longer than a night or two. My fourteen-year-old sister was too often content to sit with her nose pressed into the pages of a book for hours on end and ignored my pleas for attention.

I loved the mix of personalities that came with such a lively bunch—giggling together upstairs in bed when we were supposed to be sleeping, telling stories, sneaking downstairs for a late night snack, boys picking on the girls and vice versa.

For me, a houseful made Christmas all the more special, and at that young age I couldn't understand why Mom and Dad didn't want to comply with my request for more siblings. Little did I understand that they were reaching the twilight of their parenting years.

Married in 1929, my parents lived a simple life on a family farm in central Minnesota, homesteaded in 1886 by my dad's grandfather. By the mid-50's they had been married twenty-seven years and were active in church and 4-H activities. Their five oldest children were already married or finishing high school, and the extended family also included three small grandchildren. Other than a nine-year gap between those five and the youngest, a seven-year-old daughter, their lives were running in decidedly rural fashion.

My mom had grown up on a typical farm, the oldest daughter in a family of fourteen siblings. As was common in those days, she quit school after the eighth grade to stay home and help her mother with the younger ones, understanding the sense of duty to family. And now, after raising six children of her own, she sensed a well-deserved, slower pace within reach for the first time in her life.

And then one day an all-too-familiar feeling washed over her. *Could it really be?* That same feeling reappeared the next day…and the next. Yes, hard as it was to believe, she was expecting *another* baby. Oh, to think of starting over with baby number seven at the age of forty-nine. I can only imagine how she must have questioned the timing.

It reminds me of young Mary and how she must have questioned God when she was told of the baby soon to arrive. Can you envision her thoughts when the angel appeared to her? Then Mary said to the angel, "How can this be, since I do not know a man?" (Luke 1:34 NKJV). As the angel explained God's plan, she accepted the miraculous news immediately. Then Mary said, "Behold the maidservant of the Lord! Let it be to me according to your word" (v. 38). And the angel departed from her. What a wonderful example of her willingness and obedience to God's will for her life.

I often wondered what kinds of thoughts ran through my mother's mind while lying awake at night in their simple farmhouse, frost licking the windowpanes in the darkness of winter. Did she question God's plan for her life, believing she was too old to have a healthy baby? Too old to raise another child?

With willingness and obedience to God, she too, along with my father, selflessly accepted the responsibility of raising a "second family" in their fifties, a time when most couples were looking forward to taking it easy. In a small, rural farmhouse heated only by a wood stove and with no running water, my parents welcomed me into their simple home, placing the well-worn crib in the midst of the warm kitchen where my mother spent most of her days.

She never shared with me any of the doubts or fears she might have experienced; instead she chose to recount the wonder of it all. Retired from farming, Dad now worked in town as the City Assessor and oftentimes, it was just she and I at home since my fourteen-year-old sister spent many afternoons baby-sitting.

As soon as Mom pulled out her basket of yarn to crochet, I'd hop up on the couch next to her, watching the strand slide over her fingers, up and around the hook and back again as she fashioned the beginning of a pair of mittens. I might ask again why I didn't have brothers or sisters close in age.

Her brown eyes would light up, and she'd begin, "Did I ever tell you what the doctor said when you were born?"

And I'd nod, waiting for her to tell me again.

"Dr. Davis said to me the minute you were born," she'd say, her voice already choked with emotion. "Congratulations, Jessie...you have the most beautiful baby girl I've ever seen." My mother's expression was filled with love and warmth as she repeated the story. "And you were the most beautiful baby girl," she'd continue, unaware how her gentle spirit presented such a wonderful example to her young daughter's eyes.

Then she'd continue, "Did I ever tell you about your first Christmas when you were just a few months old?" I knew the story well. Dad drove the Chevy into town so Mom could do their shopping, and in the crisp chill of a Minnesota December, she had me bundled from head to toe. She shopped her way through the aisles of the Five and Dime Store, a favorite gathering place on Main Street especially during the bustling holiday season. "Merry Christmas, Jessie. Whose little one is this?" the other ladies would ask her. "Another grandbaby?"

"No," she'd reply, cradling the bundle tightly. "This one's mine."

"Oh, c'mon…you must be teasing," they'd laugh, knowing she was prêt-near fifty years of age!

"No," she'd insist, peeling back the blanket for a peek. "This is Barbara…and she's my daughter."

As the ladies walked away, whispering under their breath, my mother simply smiled, holding her Christmas bundle all the tighter.

SHARING CHRISTMAS

KATHRYN LAY

Help needy Christians; be inventive in hospitality.

ROMANS 12:13 THE MESSAGE

Every year new and different faces are a part of our Christmas dinner. Because early on in our marriage my husband and I found we were unable to have children, Christmas seemed lonely at times—even when we were surrounded by family. Without planning we suddenly found ourselves with an opportunity to minister and provide a special holiday gift to others who might be alone on this special day.

Several years ago we learned that a young couple in our church was unable to be with their families, far away, that Christmas. They were new in town and new in their marriage.

Expecting to spend that Christmas alone, they were thrilled when we invited them to spend the day with us. We had been married only a few years, and I had grown accustomed to our

Christmas holidays alone. Yet, their joy was such a blessing that we decided to make the Christmas invitation to our home a tradition.

Over the years, many new friends have shared our Christmas turkeys and pecan pies. The second year of our new tradition, we invited an international student from China, attending our local college. We discovered he had been in the States nearly a year. Still, our offer was his first time to be invited into an American house; his first Christmas in our country was spent in our home.

The college was empty and silent. Most American students were home with their families for the weeks in between semesters. The apartment complex that our student friend lived in consisted mainly of international students. Most were using the time to travel around the state. But he was twenty years older than most and decided to remain in town rather than go along with them. He was obviously lonely. With two years left to study in our country, his wife and children waited for him many miles away in China.

Everything was new to him that Christmas day. The extravagant meal, decorated tree, and Christmas songs on the radio had to be explained. As we do every year, my husband read the "Christmas story." Our new friend listened, eager to learn about American customs and holiday celebrations. I worried that he would not enjoy the food, but he did. He sat silently and calmly while my husband and I fought a grease fire in the oven.

I wondered if he thought this to be a part of our traditions.

One year we learned of a single friend at church who would be spending Christmas alone. He could not take the time from work he needed to visit his family in another state. We invited him to come early and spend much of the day with us. He became a part of our celebration as a family. While I ran around the kitchen putting final touches on the meal, he helped my husband start a fire in the fireplace.

After dinner, the last gift from under the tree was brought to him—his name on the tag. He felt that he was not a last-minute guest, but rather someone who was special to us. The joy of a smile spreading across his lonely face was the only gift we needed from him.

Another year we worked among a refugee church from Laos. They met every Sunday afternoon in our church building. While spending time with them, we became especially close to one young couple. Although they had lived in America for ten years, neither had spent a traditional Christmas in an American home.

Her family lived in Oregon, his in Maine. With each living half a country away from their families and their first Christmas so far from their homes, we could not stand to see them alone. They were used to holidays crowded with people, and we were happy to include them in our day.

Others we know have begun sharing their Christmas holidays as well, inviting singles, college students, single parents and their children, or seminary students to share this special meal with their family.

Hebrews 13:2 NASB tells us, "Do not neglect to show hospitality to strangers, for by this some have entertained angels without knowing it." This verse has come alive in their homes as well as ours. Their children have grown more open by meeting people of other cultures. Singles feel a part of a family. Students far from home and family make new friends on a day when the lonely feel even lonelier.

Each year after Thanksgiving we begin thinking about those who might be spending Christmas alone. We try to ask them early, so they are able to look forward to the holiday and not be alone or dreading Christmas. They know someone truly cares and desires their company. Making them feel important by asking them to bring a dessert or other part of the meal is another way we share Christmas with our guests.

Christmas is a time of reflection upon a special birth. It has traditionally become a time of giving and receiving. This is usually thought of as fighting crowded department stores to purchase an object that will be wrapped and given. Yet sharing your time, home, and family is a priceless and precious gift to your guest.

We now have a five-year-old daughter who tells everyone, "When I grow up, I want to help poor people." Her giving attitude makes it easy to invite others to our holiday table. She is making friends with the children of the many refugees and immigrants who attend our English as a Second Language classes at church.

We pray that she will continue to look forward to the new faces at our Christmas dinner table every year. And maybe, when she is grown, she will carry on the tradition in her own home.

*M*ORE THAN NEEDED

JENNIFER JOHNSON

Now to Him who is able to do far more abundantly beyond all that

we ask or think, according to the power that works within us.

EPHESIANS 3:20 NASB

"I have an extra seventy dollars worth of overtime on my check." Albert waved the paper in front of me.

"Really!" I glanced up from the pile of bills and overstretched checkbook. My young husband looked tired, really tired. Permanent bags weighed his gorgeous, sea-blue eyes. His gray and white striped work shirt was wrinkled at the bottom from hours behind the wheel of an overnight delivery truck.

"I want you to spend it on Christmas for the girls." He fell into the chair and propped up his feet.

I gazed at the numbers in the checkbook and the seventy-five-dollar electric bill in my lap. They seemed to stick out their tongues and wave at me. No matter what I did, I couldn't pay the bill. His overtime would cover it.

How did we get into this financial predicament? When we'd bought the van, we knew it would be tight, but then we added the truck payment. Foolish, foolish move. Our cars, alone, doubled our house payment.

Rubbing my blossoming belly, I wanted to cry. I'd prayed so hard for this baby, our third child. I'd begged and bargained with God to get her. In just two months she'd be here, and we couldn't make ends meet now.

I closed my eyes and thought of the advice of our Christian friend/financial counselor. "You'll have to consolidate against your house." Her words rang through my mind. "You have no choice."

Knowing she was right, I'd gone to the bank, gathered the necessary forms, and filled them out. Then, it came time to sign. "Albert, I don't think I can sign this."

"Do we have a choice?"

"Logically, no."

"Then, sign it."

I cried and sought out my God. The one thing we had was escrow. With the third child in a small starter home, I desperately wanted the opportunity to get a bigger house when the girls grew. We wouldn't always be in this financial shape. We'd just made bad choices with vehicles, really bad choices. Five years, surely we could make it through five years.

Trust me, Jennifer.

God's words could have been spoken audibly. I knew, without a doubt, we were to allow God to move with our finances. He would see us through without consolidation. We would seek Him for every penny spent.

"We got the Christmas Wal-Mart ad." Albert's voice brought me back from my reverie.

"Did we?" Oh, how I longed to take his overtime and race to Wal-Mart. I wanted my precious girls, three and six, to have everything their hearts desired, Barbies and babies, dress-up clothes, and art supplies.

"Look here," he chuckled. "We got another traveler's check for seventy-five dollars."

Tears streamed down my cheeks. That was too much. God was too good. It was the second anonymous check we'd received. I gazed at the electric bill, *just enough to pay you off.* This time I stuck out my tongue and waved.

I glanced at the Wal-Mart ad in his lap. My heart sped up, and a smile split my lips. "Can I see the ad?"

"Sure." He tossed it to me.

Toys of all kinds were to be on sale early in the morning in just two days, the day after Thanksgiving. Barbies for two dollars, babies for five, craft supplies at varying prices. This couldn't be real. Every single item I wanted to buy the girls was on sale. They were more than on sale, in my opinion; they were a specific blessing from God.

Anticipation, excitement, and an overall rush of adrenaline streamed through me as I circled one item, then another, then another. I tallied prices in my head. "You'll have to set my alarm for five in the morning."

"What?" Albert looked up from the sports section of the paper.

I grinned, nearly bouncing on the couch. "Yep. I can get each girl five presents for that seventy dollars. But, I can't take any chances. Gotta get there early."

Albert shook his head and looked back at the paper. "Whatever you say."

Just one month later, squeals woke us from our slumber. "It's Christmas, Mom! It's Christmas, Dad!"

Within moments, our three-year-old, Hayley, stood beside the bed, tugging on my sleeve. "Wake up. We gots lots of pwesents."

"Come on, y'all," our six-year-old, Brooke, jumped on her daddy's belly. "Let's open presents. Let's open presents."

My husband hopped out of bed and pulled me out as well. We walked into the living room to find Brooke divvying the presents between herself and her sister. I ran into the kitchen, grabbed the camera, and then raced back toward the excitement.

"Okay, Brooke, open one up."

She tore into the wrappings until a baby doll was exposed. "Ohhhh, she's so pretty." Brooke caressed the plastic front of the box.

"No fair, I want one too." Hayley stomped her foot and pouted.

Albert grinned. "It's your turn, Hayley."

She smiled and clapped. "Okay." She picked up one of her gifts and tore into the paper. "A Barbie," she squealed. "A Barbie! I wuv her. I wuv her. I wuv her."

"Now, you have your very own, and you won't have to use Brooke's." I took a picture of her with her treasure.

"Open it, Daddy." She ran to Albert trying diligently to rip into the plastic.

Mere moments passed, and the girls had opened each of their five presents. I sat and watched as Albert pried open Brooke's box. She stood not so patiently beside him waiting to hold her new baby doll. Hayley sat at his feet brushing her beloved Barbie's hair.

Complete satisfaction and utter awe washed over me. Once again, God had taken care of us. I rubbed my swollen tummy. My soon-to-be-born, third little girl replied with a succession of kicks. Soon, she'd make her way into this world. One more mouth to feed, one more body to clothe, one more child to love.

God would provide...more than needed.

STRUCK GOLD AT CHRISTMAS

JOAN CLAYTON

The man who finds a wife finds a treasure and receives favor from the LORD.

PROVERBS 18:22 NLT

"COME LIVE
WITH ME,
AND BE MY
LOVE, AND
WE WILL
SOME NEW
PLEASURES
PROVE. OF
GOLDEN
SANDS, AND
CRYSTAL
BROOKS,
WITH SILKEN
LINES, AND
SILVER
HOOKS."

—*John Donne*

"Hey guys! See that girl over there?" The tall, lanky kid pointed, talking to his friends.

"That fat girl in glasses eating an ice cream cone?" they asked, almost chuckling.

"Yep! That's the one," he said. "I'm going to marry her someday." (And he was talking about me.)

Everyone knew the prize "catch" of high school. He was the All State center, the track star, and so tall, dark, and handsome you wouldn't believe it. Needless to say, "zilch" became my popularity with the girls in our little country high school. Emmitt only had eyes for me.

The day after our high school graduation, Emmitt had to report for duty in the Army. We clung to each other, and I cried as I watched that big Greyhound bus carry my high school sweetheart away…until it disappeared from my vision.

Emmitt wrote faithfully during those years. He told me of his love and homesickness. Yet, not one single time did he ever mention anything about marriage. Finally, after what seemed to me to be an eternity, Emmitt's tenure in the Army ended. He arrived at Christmastime, and just seeing him again was the best gift I can ever recall. When I saw him get off that train, I gasped. *How could he be more handsome than ever?* My heart beat with excitement.

He swooped me up in his arms and turned me around and around. He began to tell me of his plans, and my joy turned to disappointment and dismay. He told me he and some Army buddies had plans for striking gold in Alaska.

I was devastated!

I hadn't planned to say it. In fact, I was shocked at what I heard coming out of my mouth.

"Will you marry me?" I screamed.

Emmitt had the most surprised look on his face. He took me in those big strong arms saying, "I thought you'd never ask."

I didn't care whether it was leap year or not. I just knew I was in love with this man!

Just like their daddy, our three wonderful sons are tall, dark, and handsome, too. I have been reaching up to hug handsome men for a long time. Now I am reaching up to hug tall, beautiful grandchildren. I feel great happiness in those same familiar strong arms around me that were inherited from their granddaddy.

Our children and grandchildren recently hosted a golden wedding celebration for us. The best part of the celebration for me happened when Emmitt took me in his arms on our golden wedding night and whispered in my ear: "Remember that Christmas when I came home from the Army and was going to Alaska to strike gold? Instead, I stayed here and struck gold."

I shall always remember that beautiful Christmas Eve. Two people made my life complete…a little baby born in a manger and a husband, both whose love I could not live without.

To tell the truth, I was the one who struck gold.

A LESSON IN FORGIVENESS

KAYLEEN J. REUSSER

As God's chosen ones, holy and beloved, clothe yourselves

with compassion, kindness, humility, meekness, and patience.

COLOSSIANS 3:12 NRSV

It was snowing as I finished unbuckling my baby from her car seat. A honk from behind reminded me that I was holding up traffic on a one-way street.

I didn't care. My six-month-old had to get an immunization shot, which meant she would be up all night with a fever. My head ached like I was coming down with the flu, and my husband's job didn't look steady for the holidays. I wasn't in a good mood.

The truck honked its horn again. When I finally had my little one in my arms and covered from the cold air, I looked up and felt my heart sink. I had inadvertently parked in a delivery zone. A look at the name printed on the truck confirmed that I was parked in its delivery zone.

Angry at myself for not noticing the sign sooner, I put my baby back into the car and looked down the street. The nearest empty place was more than a block away. Gritting my teeth, I was tempted to go home and reschedule my baby's vaccination for a day when things were going better, but I didn't.

After managing to parallel park in a tight spot, I again prepared to get out of my car. Glancing up, I saw someone waiting for me outside. I knew it was the truck driver. Bracing myself for a verbal attack, I slowly emerged from the car.

"Sorry about that back there." A strong note of apology rang in the man's voice. I looked at him suspiciously. He was actually grinning at me!

"I saw you had a baby," he continued, "but there wasn't any other place big enough for me to park in."

I managed to stammer my own apology, though I was completely taken aback by his friendly manner. Like Scrooge, I wondered if this was a setup.

"I'd like to give you this." The stranger held out a ceramic mug with his company's name on the side. He didn't wait for my reply, but shouted "Merry Christmas" and sprinted away, as fast as he dared on the slick pavement.

I stared after him, the mug still in my hand. As the snow continued to fall steadily around me, a warm feeling spread throughout my body, and I smiled for the first time all day.

At home that mug now has a permanent place on my kitchen windowsill. It serves as a constant reminder to me of the way that driver showed unexpected kindness and forgiveness to me that day. It also reminds me of the way God consistently forgives each of us even when we deserve it the least.

Seeing the mug each morning as I begin my day inspires me to work on showing that same kindness and forgiveness to everyone I encounter—clerks, cashiers, complete strangers—not just at Christmas, but every day of the year.

CHRISTMAS PRESENTS OR PRESENCE

MELINDA LANCASTER

You have made known to me the ways of life;

You will make me full of joy in Your presence.

ACTS 2:28 NKJV

When I was a child, the week before Christmas was always very exciting. Our house was decorated beautifully, and we spent time with family and friends. On Christmas Eve, I can remember being so eager for Santa to come and bring gifts.

Bedtime would come, and we would race off to bed but try to stay awake to hear something, so that we could catch a glimpse of the deliveries under our tree.

Of course, we always fell fast asleep so we never did see anything or anyone. All we knew was that when we went to bed there was nothing under the tree, and when we woke up there were beautifully wrapped presents everywhere! What fun we had opening them! We squealed with delight as we opened each present.

As the years went by, we still found the holiday season to be delightful. Instead of waiting for Christmas morning, we began a tradition of opening one present on Christmas Eve. We waited all day in anticipation of that moment. The excitement made me queasy every year for as long as I can remember.

As my siblings and I got married and had children, we found great joy in the thought that *Christmas is for kids.* We never forgot to give honor and reverence to Jesus Christ, but our joy came from the children's response to the gifts.

Something changed when my husband, son, and I moved away from our family. We made trips back at Christmas, and though the journey was long, it seemed that our focus changed from Christmas presents to being in the presence of those whom we loved. I look back on our Christmas travels, and they were very special times. Yes, we made sure that the children had presents, and we gave gifts that were tokens of our love, but the focus had shifted once again. Spending time with our loved ones and celebrating the birth of Jesus were priceless presents to us.

Then several years ago, illness began to plague me, and we were blessed to have my parents come to live near us. We no longer make the long journeys home, and our son gets to have Christmas Eve and Christmas Day at home. We never tried to sell him on Santa Claus and have tried to instill in him the real meaning of the season.

Unfortunately, I don't often feel the anticipation that I once felt about the holidays. To be honest, what I have felt recently has been pressure and some discouragement, as I cannot do many of the things I once did—things that I thought made Christmas special. But the upside is that the focus has now stopped being about presents and instead has become more about "presence"...people's presence in our lives and our presence in theirs. Above all else, it has come down to sensing a Christmas "Presence" of peace and love that can only come from Jesus.

It isn't necessary anymore to make a Christmas list, because the things I desire cannot be purchased with money. I am content with what I have, and the only thing that I desire is that sense of wonder and awe I felt as a child—not for a visit from Santa—but for my Heavenly Father. When you think about it, in some ways He parallels the myth of Santa. He knows all of His children by name. He knows the desires of our hearts and has the ability to visit each of us simultaneously. He does not leave gifts that are perishable, but if we will look for Him, He will leave something which is priceless...His Presence in our midst.

There is nothing else I need for my life. Material things no longer make me happy, and let's face it, we cannot look to people for a sense of joy. But His Presence during this holiday season is something that we are all in need of and deeply longing for.

You might ask why God's Presence is so important to me. Well, the Bible says that in His Presence is fullness of joy, in His Presence there is rest, and in His Presence is peace of mind, hope, and renewal. Most of all, in His Presence is a love even deeper than the deep love of family and friends. I guess you can see why I have stopped asking for Christmas presents and now ask for Christmas "Presence" instead.

Perhaps you feel the same way today. You might be weary or even hurting deep inside. There might be a pile of presents right there in front of you, but you find no joy, peace, hope, or love.

Sometimes all we need to do is take our eyes off those presents, and instead focus them on God's Presence—which He has promised to us even now. He will not withhold any good thing from us...and having His Presence in our lives is the best gift we could ever hope to receive.

A LIGHTHEARTED HOLIDAY

GINGER BODA

In the same way, let your light shine before men, that they may

see your good deeds and praise your Father in heaven.

MATTHEW 5:16 NIV

Our little girl, Alisha, was intent on bringing the Christmas spirit to her little gray house on Ole Susanna Street. It seemed there was a bit of "bah humbug" in the air, since some major financial burdens had pressed in on us. I tried my best to create the warmth of the holiday in our home that year, but something was definitely missing. Alisha knew exactly what was needed.

She found our old box of Christmas lights up in the rafters of the garage. Very gingerly, she began to remove them strand by strand, recalling how her dad would check each one; ensuring that they still glowed. She plugged them into the wall and smiled with each success. In the past, her father had displayed the Christmas lights on the outside of the house, but this year Alisha realized that he wasn't "getting around to it." There was just one week left before Christmas, she pondered, and it looked as though the holiday was going to come and go without even a slight glimmer twinkling from their homestead.

Alisha and her dad hadn't said much to each other lately. Oh, she knew that he loved her, but the words never came easy for him. It seemed that ever since she turned thirteen last year, she and her father had drifted apart, somewhat. He seemed to enjoy talking with her brothers because they always had sports and "guy stuff" to discuss. That was just on the surface, though, and she knew her dad felt depressed. Something in Alisha now told her that her father needed her more than he cared to admit.

I called to Alisha to come help with the cut-out cookies, but she didn't answer. Glancing down the hallway toward her bedroom door, I discerned no movement. Oh, she's probably listening to her music, I presumed. All of sudden, strange noises were heard, coming from outside the house. Distracted by the commotion interrupting his day, Mark went to the front door and listened for a moment. Shrugging his shoulders, he shuffled back to his spot in front of the television and let out a big sigh as he sat down.

I tiptoed, sock footed, out to the yard in the chilly afternoon. Looking up and straining to see if there might be a cat on the roof, I noticed the Christmas lights hemming the eves over our garage door; apparently still in their placement process. However, to my confusion, there was no one on the roof. Once again, I called towards the front door for Alisha. Slowly, a sweet little face emerged over the peak of the house. There she was, lights in one hand and stapler in the other, trying to do what has always been known in her home as a "man's job." She was grinning from ear to ear.

I gulped hard, then smiled, and praised my little girl for her efforts. However, I did suggest that she come down immediately before getting hurt. *Goodness, she's gutsy,* I thought.

Hearing the rooftop conversation from the comfort of his cozy couch, Mark reluctantly came outside to assess the situation. He eyed our little rooftop elf, but said nary a word; he simply turned slowly back toward his abode.

The spirit of Christmas was difficult to feel with the tension in the air, and the reason for the season seemed to have been forced out with the stresses. *The simple joy of being together as a family should be enough,* I pondered. My heart ached for my daughter whose efforts were to bond with and please her father.

Knowing that Alisha was determined, I retrieved my jacket from the closet and headed past the living room to the front door to assist her. I halted mid-step, and a grin quickly replaced my frown, as I surveyed my scrooge of a husband putting on his shoes and jacket. Across the room, I noticed that the television had finally lost its voice. Seizing the moment, I sauntered over to the stereo, switched on some Christmas music, and turned to face my hubby. The room began to fill with warmth as our eyes met and a knowing smile was exchanged.

In no time at all, there appeared to be all kinds of activity heard from the rooftop of the little gray house on Ole Susanna Street as the little girl and her daddy laughed and worked together. Although he clearly stated that "he was pushed into the job," he DID wink as he said it. Nothing had changed monetarily for us. Christmas presents would still be scant, but the hearts that lived in the little house were already richly gifted. It didn't take much to remind us that the light in our spirit can brighten our world, and the people we love, if we just take the effort to display it.

Finally, the spirit of love and joy had arrived just a week before Christmas. The outline of the homestead became illuminated, as did the heart of our little girl as she bonded with her father and tucked away a precious and brightly lit memory in the treasure chest of her childhood.

WHAT CHRISTMAS IS ALL ABOUT—PEOPLE HELPING ONE ANOTHER

DAVID FLANAGAN

You are generous because of your faith. And I am praying that you

will really put your generosity to work, for in so doing you will come

to an understanding of all the good things we can do for Christ.

PHILEMON 1:6 NLT

"THERE IS
NO REAL
RELIGIOUS
EXPERIENCE
THAT DOES
NOT EXPRESS
ITSELF IN
CHARITY."

—*C.H. Dodd*

Recently, my wife Linda and I found ourselves at the mall among hundreds of other parents, grandparents, aunts, uncles, and other would-be gift givers joining in the quest for the ideal present. As I wandered down aisle upon aisle of bikes, games, dolls, and Playstations, I found myself simultaneously awed and somewhat disheartened over the exorbitant cost of toys these days.

As my journey continued I experienced tremendous feelings of ambivalence toward the holiday season. On the one hand I was thrilled at the thought of buying gifts for the kids and witnessing the pleasure that such items would bring. At the same time, I was concerned about whether I would be able to afford enough gifts to ensure such pleasure.

I found myself thinking about other parents who may not have the resources to feed, clothe, or house their children, never mind smother them with gifts. What does a single, welfare mom tell her child on Christmas morning when the boy rushes over to a tree and finds that there's nothing beneath it? How does an unemployed dad respond to his child who asks, as tears well up in her eyes, what she has done that was so wrong, so terrible that no gifts were delivered to her this Christmas? What crosses these little children's minds when they visit their friend's house and notice a mountain of toys heaped beneath the tree?

While thinking about these questions I found myself drifting back to my own childhood and thinking about holidays past: including the annual Christmas Eve ritual of setting out hot cocoa and cookies for a fictitious Santa and carrots for imaginary reindeer. I remembered my little sister Patsy opening her gifts on Christmas morning and the joyful family gatherings at Nana Flanagan's.

How wonderful those Christmases were and how fortunate I am to have such pleasant, enduring memories of them.

Yet, there was one Christmas that may not have been quite so enjoyable had it not been for the generosity and compassion of one local charitable organization that helped us in the 60s when economic hardship and poor health forced my mother to request assistance.

Unless you have been fortunate enough to have received assistance from one of the many charitable organizations that exists you really cannot appreciate the wonderful service they provide. Such organizations and the volunteers who support them truly embody the holiday spirit and can make a profound difference in the lives of those dependent upon them.

Think about it—total strangers coming together, giving of their time, money, and energy to help make life a bit more bearable for people they may never meet. That to me is truly what the Christmas season is all about!

This Christmas why not consider putting aside a little bit of money for a financial contribution or possibly plan some time to volunteer or help out one of your local charitable organizations whose mission is to ensure that no one is forgotten during the holidays? The compassion and consideration you invest will be appreciated and never, ever forgotten. And best of all, you will be celebrating in the true meaning and spirit of Christmas.

LONG-DISTANCE CELEBRATION

ESTHER M. BAILEY

Now you can have sincere love for each other as brothers

and sisters because you were cleansed from your sins when

you accepted the truth of the Good News. So see to it that you

really do love each other intensely with all your hearts.

1 PETER 1:22 NLT

"LOVE
BRINGS
PEOPLE
CLOSE NO
MATTER
HOW
GREAT THE
DISTANCE."

—*Author Unknown*

The tradition of spending Christmas with my mother and grandmother continued the year after I married. However, the following year, my husband wanted to spend the holiday with his family. While I fully understood and concurred with the idea of fair play, the realization that my mother and grandmother would be alone and possibly have the Christmas blues greatly disturbed me. Somehow I felt a need to do more than send presents and make a long-distance call. It was time for me to put positive thinking to work to come up with a plan.

Words from the song, "The Twelve Days of Christmas," soon inspired me. Gifts opened on consecutive days would enhance the joy of the season, but I could still perceive the feeling of loneliness my loved ones would experience on Christmas Eve—the time when we normally exchanged gifts. I wanted to build on something that would bring meaning and something special to Christmas for them.

A plan formed in my mind. Indeed I would send each of them twelve presents designated for the twelve days preceding Christmas. Instead of opening the gifts each day, though, the ladies would open an attached envelope, read a clue, and try to guess the content of the package. I instructed them to write down the guesses to compare with the actual gifts they would open on Christmas Eve.

Money was ideal as the major gift for both women. The clue to the money tree I made for my mother read, "You always told me this didn't grow on trees, but maybe you were wrong."

Since a reward adds excitement to any game, I placed an ample supply of coins in a box labeled Bank. Each correct guess earned fifty cents. Unearned money would be donated to their favorite cause or mission.

To add nostalgia to the celebration, I composed a letter for them to read on Christmas Eve. I opened my heart and simply allowed my sentiments to spill onto the paper. Then I continued with the "I remember when" approach my mother had introduced to me while I was growing up.

I made note of all my precious memories. First I recalled when my Christmas memories began when I was nearly four years old. The set of blue metal dishes I received that year made a lasting impression on me—perhaps because I liked to throw tea parties for my dolls.

I wrote about our family traditions. While our family lived in the country, we trekked to the woods each year to cut down a Christmas tree. With strings of popcorn and a few homemade decorations added to our collection of ornaments, we trimmed the tree that provided me with hours of enjoyment.

I shared about the time when my childish wonder over presents and decorations declined—I had discovered the real meaning of Christmas. Recognizing the significance of the coming of our Savior had enhanced the celebrations our family had shared in the past at Christmas, and I hoped it would carry over this year giving us a sense of togetherness even on a long-distance basis.

As I finished my letter, I realized I had already experienced a sense of togetherness. I prayed that, although I was absent, I could project part of myself across the miles to the ones I loved. "Why don't you share some of your good memories with each other?" I challenged my mother and grandmother.

When I made my long-distance call on Christmas Day, my usually reserved mother bubbled over with enthusiasm. "It just seemed like you were here!" she said.

As it turned out, that was our last Christmas celebration free from the shadow of sorrow. My mother's health began to fail soon afterward and, a few years later, my mother and grandmother died in the same year. That is why I treasure the memory of the year I invested so much in order to share Christmas with my mother and grandmother, although we were far apart.

In one way, though, I can still celebrate Christmas with my family through faith. In coming to bring us salvation, Jesus bridged the distance between Earth and Heaven, where we shall be together again. And that is cause for the greatest celebration of all!

$\mathcal{L}$IGHTS

JESSICA INMAN

Trust in the LORD with all your heart and lean

not on your own understanding; in all your ways

acknowledge him, and he will make your paths straight.

PROVERBS 3:5-6 NIV

I press the last push-pin into the wall. I am daringly/foolishly perched on my toes on my swiveling desk chair, arranging some white Christmas lights into a lattice formation above my closet door. Some events in my life in the last few months—my birthday and college graduation, among other things—have precipitated several greeting cards from special people, and I want to display them in my room in a creative fashion.

Hopping back on the chair after retrieving the cards, I begin sliding them between the lights and the wall; some of them I leave open to reveal the words of kindness and encouragement scrawled on the inside. Upon completion, the space of wall above my closet is a visual patchwork—little squares of handwriting, an ice cream cone, a dog with a hologram bone above his sleepy head....

Plugging in the lights, the cards illuminate and sparkle.

With a sigh I ponder, *Is there something wrong with me? Because I don't know exactly what I should do next with my life?*

I graduated from college in May with absolutely no idea what I was going to do the following week. With a hodgepodge of skills and a sense of passion sketchy at best, I tried out many different options throughout the summer. I felt pulled toward compassionate ministry, youth ministry, and writing in some capacity or another, but I didn't really know how to move forward or decipher a sense of "call" amid my own personal thoughts and desires.

Thus, I found the job hunt rather complicated. I developed a résumé, applied at a student mission's organization, and made some contacts within my denomination at a budding inner-city church in another part of the state. Meanwhile, I kept my comfy position as a youth pastor's secretary.

I interviewed at the inner-city church, and eventually landed an administrative assistant position with them and informed my boss that I would be leaving after September. I also sought counsel with an urban ministry leader in my own city, who warned me that if I plunged into urban work without clarity about God's purpose in my life, the road ahead could be very hard and possibly disastrous. Deciding to heed that warning, along with the war in my stomach over the whole affair, I declined the position only a few days before I was scheduled to move.

My last day as youth group secretary just happened to be the day after the publication of my first article. My boss insisted upon taking me to lunch that day; I consented. I walked into the restaurant and thought, *Wow, the whole church office staff decided to come to lunch at the same restaurant,* not realizing this was my going away/congratulations party.

I received a card signed by the staff, a few very sweet gifts, some kudos on my article, and a bowl of baked potato soup. This was Friday; on Monday, I would have no job.

I told my boss I'd continue to help him out a little bit during the interim—they hadn't found my replacement yet, and I was happy to help him while I continued to look for something with more hours each week.

In the end, I found myself without much direction, and ended up rejoining the staff at the church permanently. To pay bills I continued to write and otherwise try to make money however I could. As much as the office staff had wished me well when I "left," they welcomed me back with even more warmth.

Looking at the spread of cards on my wall again, I survey the warm wishes and read some of the inscriptions. Gloria had written on my good-bye card, "What a beautiful young woman of God you are—both inside and out! I am really going to miss you!" On my birthday card, Mollie had written, "Your metamorphosis into adulthood has been a joy to behold." Daleen scripted, "You deserve every wonderful graduation moment." And then there was Bryan. I get a little misty-eyed reading what he—someone I had admired and sometimes felt like I had failed—admired about me.

I stand under the lights and think, *these people really seem to love me, and I don't think I understand that.*

I could tolerate lack of direction in other people. It made perfect sense to me that other people my age might struggle a little in figuring out what they were created to do the first year or two after college. But in myself, I expected more, and it was difficult to accept the seemingly aimless direction of my life. So I was thoroughly perplexed by these short messages of love and belief from my coworkers.

Perplexed, but grateful, and deeply conscious of the security God has given me through these people. Feeling their love, I can press on bravely, maybe making a couple of mistakes, but knowing that things will turn out in the end because God has gifted me in certain ways and desires to guide my life. There is an unmistakable hope in feeling loved and appreciated, and understanding that this love comes ultimately from Someone who directs my very steps.

It's getting late and yes, I should get to bed. After all, who knows what tomorrow will bring, what steps God will beckon me to take toward my future! Stepping back, I unplug the Christmas lights, hesitate a moment, then plug them back in. I may leave them on all night.

THE MUTT AND THE GOLDEN RETRIEVER

CYNTHIA SCHAIBLE BOYLL

Because you are sons, God sent the Spirit of his Son into

our hearts, the Spirit who calls out, "Abba, Father."

GALATIANS 4:6 NIV

It was a gloomy Advent for me because a lot of people I loved were going through difficult times with illness and tragic family situations. Their suffering made it hard for me to gear up for "Ho! Ho! Ho!" and frosted sugar cookies. Yet, I was mildly interested in the growing Christmas light competition between two of our neighbors. And then there was the cute Golden Retriever puppy.

The Connors, who lived two blocks from us, had tethered him in their front yard. According to school bus sources, he was an early, expensive Christmas present. Shortly after his arrival, a homely, dirty mutt began hanging around the yard with the Golden Retriever. Whenever we drove by the Connors' house, the two dogs could be seen outside sunning together. Only one was on a leash.

Not long after both of their arrivals, dozens of little flags appeared bordering the Connors' yard. My family guessed the Golden Retriever was getting invisible fencing. And we wondered if that would discourage the little stray dog.

The next day my faithful bus resources reported that the Connors had indeed gotten rid of a dog. *Poor homely mutt,* I thought, hoping that even though he was so homely that someone out there might adopt him from the animal shelter for Christmas.

The next day, what a surprise awaited my family when we drove out of our neighborhood. There, standing proudly in the Connors' yard, was the lowly mutt, bathed and groomed, with a big red collar around his neck! It seems the Golden Retriever didn't like the Connors' hospitality and had been given back to the breeders for a more suitable placement. "Smoky," however, loved his new home!

Smoky's adoption changed my entire gloomy perspective during that Christmas holiday.

Thanks to Smoky, I was reminded that none of us are orphans; we each have a special place with God and every reason to hope for a bright future. Surely the baby who had no room in Bethlehem had come to earth so there would be plenty of room for all who were needy.

I remembered the Bible verses which declare: "But when the time had fully come, God sent his Son, born of a woman, born under law, to redeem those under law, that we might receive the full rights of sons. Because you are sons, God sent the Spirit of his Son into our hearts, the Spirit who calls out, 'Abba, Father.' So you are no longer a slave, but a son; and since you are a son, God has made you also an heir" (Galatians 4:4-7 NIV).

Smoky is still in the Connors' yard, and recently I noticed he has been joined by another happy, smiling mutt, who also wears a big red collar. They remind me of a wonderful and important truth all year long.

$\mathcal{T}$O BE LOVED BY SARAH

LAROSE KARR

Therefore I also, after I heard of your faith in the
Lord Jesus and your love for all the saints, do not cease to
give thanks for you, making mention of you in my prayers.

EPHESIANS 1:15-16 NKJV

"WHAT A
WONDERFUL
LIFE I'VE
HAD! I ONLY
WISH I'D
REALIZED IT
SOONER."

—Colette

The best Christmas gift I ever experienced involved a sweet little gray-haired granny named Sarah.

I met a youthful and pregnant Sarah for the first time in 1968. She was pregnant with her fourth child.

Having recently changed schools, her daughter and I rode the school bus together when we were in the fourth grade.

Since that time, Sarah has always been surrounded by babies and children. She and I were even pregnant at the same time when I was eighteen and she was in her forties.

A few years back, she was a caregiver in the nursery at a Christian daycare. And oh, how I envied those babies. Days of nothing but loving from Sarah, how blessed those precious children were!

Sarah began attending church regularly when I was a teen. I must admit I sometimes giggled at Sarah's faith. I had never seen anyone pray before they lit an old gas cookstove. But pray she did, and light it did.

My husband and I live a thousand miles from most of our family. In the twenty years we have been away, we only went home once for Christmas. That year something happened that will forever remain in my memory. It touched a part of me deep inside, and I will always treasure the message I received.

Sarah and her husband didn't have a lot of money. They lived in an old two-story house. Her husband loved this house because it was big and roomy. It had once been a grand old home, but with time the place had been turned into two apartments, one on the top floor and the other on the bottom floor. This year they were living on the top floor.

The first night Sarah and I went into the kitchen. We began to talk, and suddenly she burst into tears. She explained they didn't have any money to pay their rent. Now Sarah had been there for me many times when I was a hurting child, and I couldn't stand to see her in distress. I went down to my van and got some of my spending money and gave it to her to pay the rent that was due.

That was the best Christmas gift I ever *gave*. She, however, gave me the best Christmas gift I've ever *received*.

Later we were sitting in the humble apartment, and I was looking at the old building. The walls were scarred and needed paint badly. The carpet was worn and stained, and truly the house had seen much better days. As I looked around the room, I thought to myself, *this is such a bad apartment. It's horrible. How can someone live in this?*

In my mind I wanted so much better for my friends. I wanted a nice place for them that had fresh paint and new furniture. And this is when I got it handed to me on a silver platter—the very best Christmas gift I've ever received.

As I sat there criticizing my friend's home in my mind, Sarah began to speak. She said in her sweet and tender voice, full of emotion, "I am so blessed. The Lord has been so good to me. I have a good family. I have a wonderful home. My life has been so full of blessings."

I can't begin to tell you how ashamed I felt. I looked at the external when I should have looked at the internal. My small amount of spending money paid her rent. My worldliness in viewing her surroundings was soon replaced by her humble attitude and gratitude to the Lord. I couldn't take back the ugly thoughts I had, but I could replace them with her gracious spirit. You see, I've known a lot of people in my life, but not many have ever given me as much love as my dear friend Sarah.

The last time I saw her, at age sixty-six, she was rocking her seven-week-old grandson and talking joyfully about the two babies she often cuddled at church. Once again I thought, *how blessed those precious children are, just as I was, to be loved by Sarah!*

HOME FOR CHRISTMAS

RICHARD C. STARGEL

with Gloria Cassity Stargel

They cried unto the LORD in their trouble,

and he delivered them out of their distresses.

PSALM 107:6

It is five o'clock in the afternoon on the 27th of December. At the Dallas/Fort Worth Airport, the terminal teems with edgy travelers studying their watches. Our little family of three maneuvers past computer screens filled with notices of cancelled and delayed flights. "That winter storm on the East Coast is causing havoc with air travel *everywhere*," I moan.

The public address system keeps up a steady stream of announcements—in Spanish, then English. Harried agents try to cope with countless questions whose answers keep changing. We reach Gate 8. "Flight 832 to Atlanta is on schedule for a 6:43 departure," I read out loud. "What a relief!" For a few moments,

I allow "visions of sugarplums" to dance in my head. Only this time, it's Mom's roasted turkey and cornbread stuffing.

"I hope we make it," my wife, Lisa, says, setting our little nine-month-old Richard down to play with his toys. "I know your parents want to see Richard enjoy his first Christmas."

"Oh, yes," I answer. "Too bad I had to work Christmas day." In my mind, I picture Mom and Dad, waiting to celebrate Christmas until the family could be together, a practice they'd started while I was on active duty with the Marine Corps. "My mother is like a mama cat with her brood of kittens," I tell Lisa, "fully content only when we are safely gathered close by."

"Why don't you call them and check on the weather in Georgia?" Lisa asks. It's hard to realize that icy conditions are paralyzing everything there, while out here we had just ridden past mesquite trees with brilliant sunshine glancing off their bare limbs.

In a few minutes, I'm back. "Mom says it's getting worse. Freezing rain and sleet are making driving hazardous. Hartsfield International reports dense fog plus air traffic already backed up due to blizzards in the northeast."

"On top of the threatening weather," Lisa adds, "it was a bit unnerving to see that television report just before coming out to the airport."

"About the unscheduled landing here this afternoon?" I silently recall the facts: *The airline jet flying from Seattle to Atlanta made an unscheduled landing due to problems with its hydraulic system used to steer the craft on the ground.*

"I'd just as soon not be reminded before we fly off into the wild blue yonder that airplanes have problems." Lisa manages a grin.

"The good news is," I reassure her, "all 228 passengers came away unharmed." I send up a hasty prayer, *Lord, please give us a safe trip home.*

As time drags on, Richard gets restless. "Lisa, if you'll stay with the bags, I'll walk him around awhile." The two of us reach Gate 15 where I chance to hear a red-coated airline employee speak with a tone of concern into his walkie-talkie: "Flight 832 has been cancelled?"

My ears snap to attention. "Did you just say Flight 832 has been cancelled? That's *my* flight!"

"Yes," he replies. "That plane is being held at its departure point. If you want to get to Atlanta tonight, you'd better get on *this* one in a hurry. Air traffic at Hartsfield is so snarled we have only a fifteen-minute window to get in there."

With that, Richard and I do an about-face and sprint off down the concourse to gather up Lisa and our gear. We hustle back to Gate 15. Flight attendants double as gate attendants. "It's open seating," they say as they rush us aboard. Inside the cavernous aircraft, we—along with a handful of other passengers—take our pick of seats. Within minutes, the plane pushes back from the gate.

We're airborne when we hear a flight attendant mention the word "Seattle." Lisa and I exchange startled looks that say, *Uh, oh! We're on the 767 that landed at Dallas this afternoon due to mechanical problems!* Of course, common sense tells me the airline would not let the plane fly if it were not ready. Still…*Dear Lord, protect us,* I pray.

My concern travels to Georgia. *I'm sure our family has learned about our cancelled flight. They're probably wondering where we are and why we aren't calling.* I picture the house, decorated from top to bottom. And on the coffee table, in its traditional place of honor, is our unique nativity scene—unique because it consists of only two figures. The Bible is opened to the Christmas story in Luke, chapter 2. Just in front of that, there is a small ceramic figure of the Christ Child. Watching over Him—lovingly, prayerfully—is His mother.

By now, *my* mother is peering out the window for the hundredth time, worrying about the weather and praying we'll get a flight out and a safe trip home. *Please, Lord....*

About ten o'clock, aboard the 767, the "Fasten Seatbelts" lights flash on. The captain announces, "We're making our final approach into Hartsfield." I look out the window. Fog is so thick our landing lights bounce back at us off the mist. A runway is nowhere to be seen. I pray the hydraulic system is in good working order, and then listen for the lowering of landing gear. *Thump. Groan. Grind.* Perfectly normal sounds, I tell myself. But I admit that my breath catches as the wheels impact the runway. They hold. Whew! *Thank You, Lord.*

We spill out into the terminal at Hartsfield International and locate a pay phone to call home. "Mom?"

"Where *are* you?" she asks, sounding relieved to hear my voice. "Back at your apartment in Texas?"

"No, ma'am, we're at the Atlanta airport."

"But you can't be!" Mom exclaims. "We've talked with the airline several times. There was not another flight coming in tonight! How in the world did you get here—on a *phantom flight?*"

"You're not going to believe it," I say, somewhat in awe myself. "I'll tell you the whole story when we get home."

We collect our rental car and cautiously head north on I-85 for the fifty-mile drive to Gainesville. In his car seat, travel-weary Richard falls sound asleep. Picking our way through thick fog and treacherous black ice on the highway, I hear the radio announcer report road closings and power outages and poor visibility. On the open road, our headlights occasionally pierce the grayness to reveal tall, skinny pine trees bending almost to the ground, their needles coated with ice.

At long last, we're almost home, and I replay in my mind the events of the past several hours. "You know, Lisa," my voice breaks the silence; "if I hadn't been walking Richard we wouldn't have caught that plane. We'd still be in Texas."

"And Richard would be terribly out of sorts by now," she adds.

"Yes. And think how, when we needed a plane to Atlanta, one was sitting there—completely unplanned—ready to take off. And an almost *private, gigantic* plane, at that!"

"Besides," I go on, "our original flight would have been in a much smaller plane, possibly ill-equipped to land under such adverse weather conditions. *This* one carried all the latest sophisticated equipment!"

"Rick," Lisa responds, "I think we just received a very special Christmas gift—maybe even a miracle!"

"I think you're right."

At 12:45 in the morning, tired but safe, we pull into the driveway. All lights of the house are on—both outside and inside. The front door swings open, and out rush Mom, Dad, and my brother, Randy, along with the aroma of holiday spices, baking turkey, and burning logs in the fireplace.

In the living room, we become a Christmas-card scene with more hugs and laughter, a roaring fire, bright twinkling lights on the tree, and tinkling bells playing *Silent Night, Holy Night.*

And on the coffee table, the tiny ceramic figure of Mary beams down on her babe in the manger. *Yes, it is good to be home!*

Thank You, Jesus, I say silently from my heart. I join the others around the tree, and then do an about-face toward the little nativity scene. "Oh, and Sir," I whisper, "HAPPY BIRTHDAY!"

LAURA'S CHRISTMAS SURPRISE

ANNE CULBREATH WATKINS

And we have known and believed the love that God hath to us. God is love;

and he that dwelleth in love dwelleth in God, and God in him.

1 JOHN 4:16

"What in the world?"

My husband Allen and I stared at the brightly decorated Christmas tree standing in the living room. I hadn't had the heart to set it up earlier, and it certainly hadn't been there when we went to bed the night before. Our astonished eyes took in the big piles of beautifully wrapped gifts waiting beneath it, and the Christmas stockings that dangled from hangers nearby. "Laura must have done all this when she came in from work last night," I guessed.

Like a couple of excited kids, the two of us prowled around under the tree, picking up and shaking each gift. "I never heard a thing," Allen said. "Did you?"

"Not a sound," I replied. Our daughter Laura worked second shift, and I always made sure to listen for her car in the drive each night. "Last night, though, I must have been asleep to the world to not have heard any of this."

Favorite family Christmas decorations were scattered around the room, and strings of colorful lights blinked cheerily from the tree. Each gift bore a tag filled out in Laura's unique handwriting, and sweet messages were scrawled on several. How she managed to set up the tree and wrap all those gifts without waking either of us mystified me. Unexpected delight filled my heart, and I wondered if this was how Laura felt at Christmastime when she was growing up.

I had always tried to make Christmas special for her, and many times I went to extreme lengths to get the things she had put on her wish list. One year it was a nearly impossible to find a purple bicycle with unicorns on it, and another time it was a roller skating stuffed dog with long blonde ears that matched Laura's hair. And each Christmas morning, the delighted expressions on her bright, beaming face made all the efforts worthwhile.

Somewhere along the way, though, I stopped looking forward to the holidays. Hard years of financial difficulties and several family deaths had dimmed my Christmas joy. Struggle though I might, nothing helped, and I greeted each holiday season with a certain dullness of spirit that kept me from enjoying much of anything. I didn't want to decorate the house or go shopping for gifts, and putting up the tree was a chore I put off as long as possible each year. Many times I prayed for the strength to get through the season, but somehow it seemed as though my prayers never got any further than the ceiling.

But now this! I was completely overwhelmed by the decorated tree's sudden appearance in the living room and the piles of gifts heaped beneath. A bit of the choking depression melted away as the warmth of Laura's thoughtfulness took hold. For the first time in years, I realized that I was looking forward to Christmas morning!

Eventually the big day arrived, and we excitedly tore into the piles of presents. I found everything from the wish list Laura had insisted I fill out and give her, along with a few special surprises. A lovely black handbag, a silver jewelry box, and one of my favorite movies emerged from the cheery gift wrap. There was even a box of thirty diskettes! And she hadn't forgotten Allen, either.

At nearly 6' 4," he can be difficult to buy clothing for, but somehow Laura managed to find two pair of blue jeans in just the right size. "Go try them on," she urged. Allen gave her a bear hug, and then disappeared down the hall with the pants. Laura and I happily examined our gifts as we waited.

Finally, Allen strode into the living room, clad in a tee shirt and a pair of the new jeans. "Look!" he commanded.

Laura and I glanced up, admired the jeans, then began chattering again. "No," Allen cried, gesturing dramatically toward the floor. "Look!"

We stared at his feet, and then burst into laughter. One hem dragged the floor, the other hit somewhere above his ankle. "Honey, they'll be fine," I managed to gasp, "as long as you stand sideways on a hill!"

As we dissolved into hysterical giggles, Laura ran for the camera and snapped a few shots of Allen modeling his mismatched hems. The last little bit of ice melted from my heart, and I brushed tears of joy and laughter from my eyes. The sadness of the past vanished as Laura's thoughtful Christmas surprise managed to help heal the part of me that years of struggling along on my own had not. Through her actions, God used her to touch my heart, and God's love uplifted my broken spirit and restored the joy of the season in my life.

$\mathcal{T}$HE GIFT OF GIVING

PAULA L. SILICI

Every man according as he purposeth in his heart, so let him give;

not grudgingly, or of necessity: for God loveth a cheerful giver.

2 CORINTHIANS 9:7

It was mid afternoon on Christmas Eve day when I found myself suddenly summoned to the phone. "Paula? This is Marie."

Uh oh, I thought. *Marie sounds stressed. Something's happened.*

"Hi, Marie. What's up?" I asked, eyeing my six dozen half-finished Christmas cookies I'd been decorating, somewhat stressed myself for lack of time. I glanced out the window, gripping the phone a little tighter. The snowstorm had passed, but the wind was howling and thick drifts of snow blanketed the ground.

"I'm kind of in a bind," Marie said, a bit breathless. "Timmy's hurt. He slipped on a patch of ice."

"Oh, no! I hope it's nothing serious."

"We don't know yet, but his ankle is swollen, and the doctor wants to see him immediately. But the thing is, I've got two church Christmas gift baskets still to deliver before dark to a couple of families in Five Points."

Leave it to Marie, I grumbled silently in my mind. *Always leaving things until the last minute. Those baskets should have been delivered yesterday.*

"So, uh, do you think you could take over for me and deliver the baskets? They're all ready to go. I could drop them by your house on my way to the doctor's. The names of the families, their addresses, and directions are stapled to the basket ribbons."

What could I do? Marie might be unorganized, but she was a very dear friend who'd always been there for me in my times of need. I had twenty relatives coming for Christmas dinner tomorrow, and tonight I had my own family of four to feed and get organized for the annual Christmas Eve Pageant. I hadn't keyed in any spare time for emergencies.

Up until Marie's call, I'd been pretty much on schedule. After all, I'd made time yesterday to deliver my own set of baskets. Judgmentally, I figured Marie should have been more conscientious and done the same.

"Sure," I said, slowly, telling myself this was Christmas, after all, the season for giving of one's self. I heard a huge sigh of relief at the other end of the line. That sigh made me feel guilty for being uncharitable, so I quickly added, "But I've got to pick up Marc from basketball practice now, so why don't you just leave the baskets out of sight on your porch? I'll pick them up, and Marc and I will deliver them."

"I owe you big time. Say a prayer for Timmy, okay?"

"I'm on it. I'll say one for you, too. Is there anything else I can do?"

"No, thanks. Just take care of the basket deliveries for me. I'd hate to think of those families going without this Christmas because of me."

"Don't worry about anything, Marie. God's in control."

God's in control, I said to myself over and over again as my fifteen-year-old son Marc and I slipped and slid our way toward downtown Denver on snow-laden streets. Marc was not in a cheery mood. His team had lost the final game by one point just before the buzzer sounded. He hadn't wanted to come with me on the deliveries; he'd wanted to go straight home to brood.

"I hate driving in snow," I said, trying to get Marc's mind off the game. Tightly clutching the steering wheel, I eased to a stop at a red light, feeling my tires slip on a patch of ice. "I wish the roads were in better shape."

Marc spun the basketball in his lap and scowled. "And I wish you'd dropped me home first," he grumbled. "I've got a lot more important things to do, you know, than go and visit some stupid needy family."

Having come to a safe stop without rear-ending the car in front of me, I turned up the volume on the radio and began to hum along. "I just love 'The Little Drummer Boy,' don't you?" I asked, trying to shelf Marc's lousy attitude for a later time. But inside, my heart sank. Lately, Marc had been a bit difficult, and his teenage selfish ways were beginning to wear on me.

My husband and I had actually started to feel inadequate as parents. Even though all Marc's life we'd tried to teach him and his brother by word and action about the joyous, intangible gifts one always receives in return for selfless giving, Marc just didn't seem to be getting the message.

I'd tried to explain how important these gift baskets were to the families who would be receiving them, how without them, there would be no Christmas at all for those children. I also had explained Marie's emergency dilemma, but he didn't want to hear it. All he could think about these days was basketball and winning. He was consumed with thoughts about his team losing another game that afternoon. I didn't like what I was hearing, nor did I like what was happening in general with Marc these days, but now was just not the right time to confront the issue.

Just before the light turned green, I asked Marc to read me the directions to the first house. It was only a couple of blocks away. Saying a silent prayer, this time for Marc that the Lord would somehow change his heart, I maneuvered the car down the street.

When we pulled up, the dingy, run-down little apartment building glared back at us, as if warning us we'd better just turn around and go away. Determined, I grabbed the first basket and began to exit the car. Marc didn't move.

"Aren't you coming?" I asked impatiently. This was not an exemplary show of Christmas spirit on my son's part, and his Scrooge-like attitude was really beginning to annoy me.

"I'd rather wait in the car," came his glum reply.

"Fine," I huffed, slamming the door shut and clutching the heavy basket as if my life depended on it.

In no time I'd entered the apartment and handed over the basket to a young mother with three children whose courage, thanks, and simple eloquence during our brief exchange had left me emotional and humbled. Back in the car, I was determined that Marc would go with me into the home on the next delivery.

The second address seemed even shabbier than the first, but undaunted, I exited the car and reached for the second basket lying on the back seat. "Come on, Marc," I said. "You're coming with me this time."

My no-nonsense tone and Mother-means-business glare got Marc's attention. "Move," I said, brooking no arguments. He skulked out of the car in silent obedience, and when he took the lead up the recently shoveled walkway I smiled secretly. I'd caught him so off guard, he'd forgotten to leave the basketball behind.

"Mr. Gonzalez?" I asked, when a man answered after the third knock.

"Sí. I am Thomas Gonzalez."

"I'm Paula Silici from Southwest Christian Church, and this is my son, Marc. We've come with some Christmas gifts for you."

Four miniature versions of Mr. Gonzalez excitedly gathered around the man's legs and peered through the door, their dark eyes huge as they perused the bulging, colorfully decorated Christmas basket I held, complete with festive greenery and tied with a fluffy red velvet bow. A woman, whom I assumed was Mrs. Gonzalez, brought up the rear.

"Please, come in out of the wind and cold," Mr. Gonzalez said as the woman shooed the kids back inside so Marc and I could enter their home. After firmly shutting the door behind us, he introduced us to his wife, Juana, and their four children—all boys.

"Merry Christmas to all of you," I said, handing over the basket and trying to keep a smile on my face as I glanced around the tiny dwelling. The living room was nearly void of furniture, except for a battered and torn couch and coffee table placed against a far wall. There were a few inexpensive but colorful posters decorating the dingy walls, but that was about it. No TV. No stereo. No live plants to cheer things up. Not even a Christmas tree, just a couple of strands of Christmas lights rimming the front window with half the bulbs unlit.

I stole a peek toward Marc who'd been cornered by the little boys. I could tell he was having a hard time, just as I was, coming to terms with the obvious poverty we were seeing, but he had laughter in his voice and a twinkle in his eyes as he teased the younger children playfully. Marc loved little kids. The oldest boy, who looked to be about ten or eleven, had hero worship in his eyes for my son who was wearing his high school letter jacket and carried a basketball.

We exchanged pleasantries for a while, though it hadn't been my intent to stay very long. Soon I sensed it was time to leave the Gonzalez family to their Christmas Eve. We would allow the family to open their basket of food and small wrapped gifts for the children in private.

When Juana and Thomas each gave us a hug good-bye, both had tears in their eyes. "Thank you. Thank you so much," they kept saying over and over again. "Please thank the church for us. Merry Christmas!"

"Merry Christmas," Marc and I chimed back as I felt my emotions climb to an all-time high. Marc, I saw, kept turning his face away, clearly trying to hold his own tears at bay.

As Thomas opened the door, Juana pressed a small card into my hand. "This is for you," she said. The card depicted the image of Jesus, the light of the world. "We know that it is because of Jesus that you have come. You and Marc have been the answer to our prayers. We do not care so much for ourselves, but for the little ones...well, we are so thankful."

"I understand," I said as a tear fell, barely missing the card as it splashed onto my wrist. With deep emotion I said, "Jesus' birth is the greatest gift of all. I will treasure this, Juana. Always."

Dusk was falling as Marc and I climbed back into the car and headed for home. Silently, I flicked on the headlights and cranked up the heater. Neither of us spoke for a long time.

Finally, I looked over at Marc and said, "Your basketball! Where is it? You must have left it back at the Gonzalez's. Do you want me to turn around?" Marc turned toward the window. I realized he was still gripped with emotion and didn't want to face me.

"What is it, honey?" I asked. "Are you okay? I don't mind going back—"

He sniffed and wiped a sleeve across his eyes. "I gave it to George, the oldest kid. He's never ever had a basketball of his own, Mom." He sniffed again. "When you told me I had to come...I didn't realize...Mom, I'm so sorry."

Lord, I prayed, *we simply cannot outgive You, can we? Who would have thought when I said yes to Marie that things would turn out this way? Thank You for doing a great work in Marc's heart today. And in my own. Something tells me this is going to be the merriest Christmas ever!*

CANDY COATED CHRISTMAS

THERESE MARSZALEK

How sweet are Your words to my taste, sweeter than honey to my mouth!

PSALM 119:103 NKJV

I admit it. I'm addicted to peanut M&M's™. My addiction is usually in remission, but I tend to relapse during the holidays. I have to resist the urge to sprint to the buffet table when friends or family select peanut M&M's™ as part of their predinner snack spread at holiday gatherings. And after fall harvest parties I've been known to cajole my kids into sharing the peanut M&M™ portion of their candy loot with dear old Mom—it was no small day when I discovered that not one of my three children liked nuts.

I was in the throes of my addiction yet again this Christmas. While perusing the Sunday newspaper one morning, I discovered an advertisement highlighting a one-day

Christmas sale at a local toy store. Oodles of toys were on special that day. My eyes widened when I spotted the best part of the enticing ad: M&Ms™, plain or peanut—$1.49—while supplies last.

My mouth watered. These weren't the measly little bags containing a mere five or six, but instead the scrumptious 14-ounce bags, large enough to easily keep an addict happy for weeks!

A bargain shopper at heart, I could hardly believe my eyes. I had long memorized M&M™ prices and knew the 14-ounce bags normally cost twice the price that this inviting toy store advertised. How could one resist such a temptation? At such a bargain, I felt justified in buying some for myself, a self-indulgence I normally wouldn't consider.

Knowing this steal would only be in effect while supplies lasted, I headed off to the toy store early in the morning on the day of the sale. Strolling up and down aisles on my M&M™ search, I finally located my coveted candies. I nabbed four of the five bags left in the display, the maximum purchase allowed.

Returning home, I stashed all four bags in my underwear drawer, my normal hiding spot for special treats. It was the only place my candy-lover children would never think of. I had no intention of sharing my secret, or my treasure, with anyone.

The next day I opened a bag of the holiday-colored delights and poured them into my crystal candy dish. Although I wasn't originally planning to share my M&Ms™, I felt convicted to allow our expected dinner guests to partake of at least one bag.

After a long day of cooking, entertaining, and cleaning up, I retreated to the living room and made a beeline for the bookshelf on which I had only hours earlier left an overflowing dish full of red and green treats.

There it was. Empty. Not one measly M&M™ was left behind. I plodded up the stairs and drew a hot bubble bath, still licking wounds of disappointment. I felt so cheated. *Oh well,* I thought. *I still have three more bags.*

The next day my fourteen-year-old son, James, told me that his school had planned a gift exchange for their Christmas party. Although he had already purchased a great gag gift, he wanted to give another gift that his fellow classmate would enjoy.

"Well? Do you know of anything he likes?" I asked as we brainstormed a possible solution.

"Oh yeah, Mom," he said. "Everybody knows Chad loves M&Ms™. Any kind. Plain or peanut, he buys them out of the candy machine at school all the time."

Oh great, I thought. *There goes my next bag of M&Ms™.*

"I have a large bag of peanut M&Ms you can give him if you want to," I halfheartedly suggested. "I guess it would be nice to give Chad something he really likes."

"Thanks, Mom," James said. "I think I'll take you up on that." Pulling my second bag of delectable treats from my secret drawer, I wrapped Chad's gifts and set them under the Christmas tree. I felt relieved knowing I still had two bags hidden for myself.

While wrapping presents later that week, I discovered some just in case gifts I had purchased but hadn't decided who to give them to. God spoke to my heart, prompting me to make a gift basket for a family in our church. Using a large wicker basket, I included a pudgy stuffed Christmas bear, a unique tree ornament, cinnamon-scented candles, flavored hot chocolate packets, and other various goodies. I tried to cleverly arrange the treats, but ended up with an empty spot regardless of how I arranged the gifts in the basket.

Thinking of this church family's three young boys, a thought popped into my mind. *I'll bet the boys would like one of those bags of peanut M&Ms™.* I pushed the thought out of my mind. *After all,* I thought, *there are plenty of other goodies in the basket. They don't really need the M&Ms™ too.*

Yes, they do. The still small voice of the Holy Spirit was undeniable.

"Fine, Lord," I said out loud. I opened my drawer, grabbed the M&M™ bag, and poured it into a decorative candy container, secretly wishing there would be leftovers. No such luck. The bag emptied, filling the dish exactly to the brim. I popped the cork top on the container, and then carefully placed it in its obvious spot in the basket. *Well,* I thought. *At least I have one bag left to enjoy.*

The first Christmas basket turned out so beautifully that I decided to create a second one. The thought of blessing another family who had faced great trial in recent months warmed my heart. Gathering more gifts together, I began building my next Christmas creation.

After putting finishing touches on the basket, the familiar voice of the Holy Spirit whispered, *And?*

"Of course," I said. "My last M&M™ bag." Opening my secret stash drawer one final time, I pulled out my last bag of precious peanut M&Ms™. After arranging it in the basket, I tied wrap around the package and topped it off with a bright red ribbon.

Smiling, I admired the two gift baskets. Anticipating the surprise for these families on Christmas Eve, I scooped the baskets up and headed to the Christmas tree. Seeing my coveted M&Ms™ nestled snuggly in between the other gifts, I checked my heart. *Am I obeying God with the right heart, or am I pouting because my M&Ms™ will soon be enjoyed by others instead of by me?*

As it turned out, delivering those gift baskets on Christmas Eve turned out to be the most enjoyable activity of the entire holiday season. Although I had privately intended to enjoy the abundance of bargain peanut M&M's™ I received great joy knowing my little sacrifice had been a blessing to others.

My candy-coated sacrifice gently reminded me of the great sacrifice Jesus made for me when I was so undeserving. He willingly came to Earth from His Heavenly home and sacrificed His life so that I might be forgiven of sin and live an abundant, eternal life.

Suddenly my M&Ms™ seemed so insignificant.

RANCO—
A GIFT FROM GOD

MARTHA CURRINGTON

There is a friend that sticketh closer than a brother.

PROVERBS 18:24

"Oh no!" I exclaimed loudly while searching through my kitchen grocery cabinet. "What's wrong?" my husband, Tom, called out from the living room.

"I forgot to buy dry black-eyed peas to cook for dinner today! I've always eaten them on New Year's Day for good luck in the New Year. Now what will we do?"

No comment from the living room. *Oh well, guess he's engrossed in the Rose Bowl football game! Think I'll make homemade vegetable and beef soup, and bake cornbread. I can just throw some purple hull peas from the freezer into the pot. Hope that suffices!* It suddenly dawns on me *I haven't written my New Year's resolutions either! What will the South think of me?*

Yet it didn't really matter. As I washed and prepared the meat and vegetables I thought about what probably caused me to forget to buy the peas; then it seemed insignificant that we would not be eating black-eyed peas today. You see, my best friend was ill, taking a turn for the worse the day after Thanksgiving—my best friend being my fourteen-year-old white Maltese named Franco.

He had developed severe, age-related, health problems. The vet had given us little hope, but with new medications being given, Franco made a rebound. I was so happy. Later the vet said he might make it to another Christmas—this Christmas. I gave Franco lots of love and attention, spending quality time with him. Then came the setback after Thanksgiving. I knew I had to be there for him; he had always been there for me.

This friendship began more than ten years ago while I was still in the grieving process from my first husband's sudden and unexpected death, heart failure at the age of forty-seven. He had died in his sleep. It was almost more than I could bear. I had lots of friends and loved ones around, but during the quiet, lonely times I needed more. I read the Bible and prayed as usual, well actually more. But I needed something physical and alive, to touch, love and care for, and to love me back. Thus, Franco came into my life via the local animal shelter, a gift from God. We both needed each other.

The recovery process began. I let him sleep on the bed beside my feet. If I was lying awake worrying, he seemed to sense it and he would come up beside me. He diverted my attention from my concerns. Then he would lay back down by my feet and I was able to drop off to sleep. Thus the close bonding began. How I thanked God for my comforting little friend! During the hot summer months, Franco slept on the linoleum covered floor beside my bed. He stayed cooler there.

Four years later I married again. Franco then had the roam of a big, out in the country, unfenced yard. A dog's life at its best!

During the Christmas season, Franco was especially a pleasure to have around. He watched as I sorted brightly colored ornaments, then hung them on the tree. He seemed fascinated by the multicolored lights blinking in rhythm with the Christmas music. And he always managed to get silver icicles draped across his coat, held in place by his very curly tight tail.

"Come on, Franco. It's time to get our picture taken by the tree." I would call out. I have a photo from each Christmas.

When it came time to wrap the gifts, he was active there too, helping the cat, Squeaky, hold the paper down, even if we were tugging to free it.

Never meeting a stranger, he was the first to greet guests when they walked in the front door.

My ailing mother also loved Franco. She called him "Frankie." After she suffered a major stroke, which left her right side paralyzed, she became bedridden. I was her primary caregiver. Franco would often lay by her bed during the day, and knowing he was there was a comfort to her. Sometimes I'd lift him up so she could pet him. Her eyes would light up and sparkle as he nestled close to her. When she passed away, it seemed that he grieved too. We exchanged mutual comfort again.

Now that Franco was in his last days, I wanted to be there for him. And I was. I didn't go anywhere unless necessary. I gave him his medications, held him close, and did my best to keep him comfortable. In the early hours of Friday, December 5, 2003, my sweet little Franco died and my husband buried my little friend in a shady spot on the outer edge of our backyard. Every once in a while I glance through the kitchen window while I'm cooking supper, smile, and think about my fluffy, devoted, little friend.

This year, I was later than usual addressing Christmas cards and buying gifts. And it took awhile for me to muster the spirit of the holiday and get into the mood for shopping, but I, half-heartedly, made it in time.

But the preparing for New Year's was a different story. *Eating dry black-eyed peas and making New Year's resolutions, well, maybe next year,* I thought.

I've discovered that God meets our individual needs in ways that best suit us. In my case, Franco was the perfect answer to help me get through the grieving, and into the healing process. The Bible states that God created everything for a reason, and in this case, it's true what we've always heard, "Dog is man's best friend." Or, in my case, "Dog is woman's best friend, at Christmastime, or anytime." And I still say, "Thank You, Lord, for the gift of Franco."

WHEN A CHILD IS BORN

DAVID FLANAGAN

You have filled my heart with greater joy

than when their grain and new wine abound.

PSALM 4:7 NIV

"All across the land dawns a brand-new morn, this comes to pass when a child is born," words from one of my favorite Christmas songs, "When a Child Is Born" sung by the great Johnny Mathis. Those magnificent words no doubt have a special meaning for anyone who has ever had the pleasure of witnessing the birth of a child, and for me those words were never quite as meaningful as the night my son, David, was born.

Each year as the holiday season approaches, I find myself thinking about family gatherings at Nana Flanagan's house, watching *It's a Wonderful Life* more times than I care to admit, and of course that most memorable of nights, December 24th, 1988. The night my first son, David, was born.

David made his grand entrance into the world at 7:23 PM on Christmas Eve, twenty-five days before his estimated time of arrival. Trust me, the last place that Linda and I expected to be that night was in the delivery room of a hospital in Boston. Earlier that day Linda had complained about her stomach and was concerned that her aches might be labor pains.

Since Linda and I had been to a party the night before and had eaten far more than our fair share of the Christmas goodies, I too had awakened with stomach pains. As a result, we were thoroughly convinced that Linda's pains were not related to her pregnancy. After all, David wasn't due until January 18th, and we had another party to go to that night.

Even so, several hours later Linda and I found ourselves checking into the hospital, and by nightfall David had arrived!

The birth of a child is indeed one of the most incredible wonders of the world, and I will never, ever forget the first time that I laid eyes on my son. Like all new parents, I found myself anxiously counting his fingers and toes and wondering if he would be a healthy baby. *How could something this magnificent happen to me,* I marveled as the nurse handed David over to me.

There he was, all six pounds, four ounces of him, crying and squirming around in my arms. David looked so small and vulnerable as I held him that I was afraid I might somehow squeeze just a bit too hard and hurt him. *How wonderful,* I thought, *to be here on Christmas Eve with my new son, holding him snugly in my arms.*

Within moments of David's birth my feelings of happiness turned to fear as the doctors and nurses began working on Linda who was apparently experiencing some type of complication from the delivery. I cannot recall ever feeling so alone and powerless as that night, standing there holding my son in my arms while my wife was lying in danger nearby.

I demanded to know what was wrong, and one of the doctors suggested I leave the room so that they could attend to Linda. Reluctantly, I left the delivery room and watched anxiously through the tiny window praying to God that everything would be okay.

The nurses were also concerned for David's health and rushed him to the Neonatal Intensive Care Unit for observation.

Embedded in my mind is the memory of sitting in a rocking chair, well into the night, holding David and trying to fight back the tears as I thought about all that had occurred. *God, please help me,* I thought, *it's not supposed to be like this.*

Tonight was supposed to be the happiest night of my life, but in moments it had become an evening of despair.

Slowly moving back and forth, holding David, and looking at him lying there so peacefully, I could hear "Oh Holy Night" playing gently through a speaker behind me. The music was so low that I could barely hear it, yet the words "Oh Holy Night, the stars are brightly shining, it is the night of our dear Savior's birth" were never more clear or poignant to me.

I continued to rock well into the night, holding David, tears streaming down my face. I prayed that Linda would make it through that night, and by God's grace she did.

Each Christmas Eve, as I look at David, his brother Evan, and my wife, Linda, I thank God for His hand, which has always been upon us and for all the many ways He continues to bless and enrich my life.

*W*HERE DID PRINCE CHARMING GO?

LINDA RONDEAU

Many waters cannot quench love; rivers cannot wash it away.

SONG OF SONGS 8:7 NIV

He opened his Christmas gifts first, then dancing with anticipation handed me my present. The gift bag was securely closed with a ridge of scotch tape, evidence of his own hand in this artful presentation. I exercised all the preopening rituals: gently stroking the outside, carefully shaking it near the ear, and complimenting the packaging, as well as the obligatory, "Thank you, Honey." I even ventured a few guesses.

"Jewelry?"

"No."

"Well, judging by the shape, it's probably not candy."

"You're right. It's not candy."

"LET ME NOT TO THE MARRIAGE OF TRUE MINDS ADMIT IMPEDIMENTS. LOVE IS NOT LOVE WHICH ALTERS WHEN IT ALTERATION FINDS, OR BENDS WITH THE REMOVER TO REMOVE."

—William Shakespeare

"Pajamas! Silk, right?"

"No. It's not pajamas, but you're getting closer. Go ahead. Open it."

In an instant, I popped the row of scotch tape and looked inside the satiny red wrapping bag. I froze in disbelief as I stared at what my husband deemed the perfect gift—A SHOWER MASSAGE! I was thoroughly convinced the romance in our relationship was more than dead. It was beyond resuscitation. In fact, it was stone cold.

"For me?" I feigned pleasure.

"Well, it's really for the both of us. That's why I spent a little extra."

Since we bought a video camera as a mutual Christmas present to each other, we set a personal gift limit of $25. He went over the top to $30.

"You shouldn't have," I said honestly.

"I know you said you wanted jewelry. Surprised?"

"Oh, yes. I'm speechless!"

At some point over the past couple decades, the Prince Charming I married went through a metamorphosis. So much so, I was starting to dread the future. *Can I really stand twenty-five more years of this?*

The handsome suitor who used to buy me Russell Stover™ Chocolates had now emerged an aged athlete peddling Mr. Coffee™. When had practicality replaced sentimentality? I wanted to tell "Mr. Baseball" to take a hike, find my misplaced fairy godmother, and tell her to bring back my Prince Charming.

Meanwhile, "Mr. Baseball" was waiting for my reaction. I muttered a halfhearted, "Gee. Thank you."

"Pour yourself another cup of coffee and relax while I get the shower massage ready for you." He took the monstrosity from the bag; and with his toolbox in hand, bounded up the steps like a schoolboy at recess.

The sounds of contented whistling could be heard downstairs while I stared into my coffee hoping to find some definition of middle-aged wedded bliss. I stewed in my disappointment. "A shower massage. Ump!" I felt like Grumpy trying to play the part of Happy.

"All set," he beamed. "You first! After all, it is your present."

"That it is." I trudged to the upstairs bathroom, took off my robe, and stepped into the widespread spray. To my pleasant surprise, the steamy mist enveloped my senses. I felt as if I had just entered a sauna.

Well, now. This is nice. I let my mind drift, imagining I was under a waterfall in Tahiti. *Hey,* I thought. *This is not bad. Not bad at all.*

Maybe he wasn't so far off the mark after all, I mused.

When there was no more hot water, I reluctantly turned the shower off, towel-dried, put on my bathrobe, and wandered downstairs.

"Mr. Baseball" was anxiously awaiting the umpire's verdict. "Well?" He looked like an innocent child who had just given his mother a wilted dandelion, waiting for a hug of gratitude.

"It's out of the ball park, Slugger. A grand slam home run."

He smiled his cute little boy smile. Behind his youthful grin, I saw the beam of love in his eyes. I recognized the faded but familiar royalty with whom I fell in love so many years ago.

I lifted my heart toward Heaven. *Thank You for my mate, Lord.* Prince Charming still lived inside that paunchy but adorable man, and he knew exactly what this tired, achy body needed.

$\mathcal{T}$HE YEAR OF THE PONY

CANDY NEELY ARRINGTON

But their trust should be in the living God,

who richly gives us all we need for our enjoyment.

1 TIMOTHY 6:17 NLT

"I'm not having a Christmas tree this year. There is no reason to go to all the fuss and trouble when I'm here alone. I don't need a tree."

With that declaration, the tiny white-haired woman turned her walker around with a thump, thump, thump as she slowly pivoted her arthritic knees to follow. Her breathing was short as she labored across the hardwood floor.

"It just won't seem like Christmas," I argued.

"Christmas has never been the same since Ed died," she countered. Giving up for the moment, I planted a kiss on her wrinkled brow and told her good-bye. Almost as an afterthought, I asked if there was ever a Christmas in her lifetime when she asked for something and didn't receive it.

She thought as the mantle clock ticked. "I asked for a pony once, when I was a young girl. I never got it."

In the days that followed, I tried to understand why I felt it important for her to have a Christmas tree. Having nothing at all in the house to remind her of Christmas seemed too sad and depressing. Without a tree, there was no place to leave her gifts, nothing to light up the corners of her dark house. I wanted to do something to brighten her life.

In my mind, I kept coming back to the pony. She might not want a tree this year but somewhere in her mind was a disappointed little girl longing for a pony. I felt a smile curl my lips as an idea took shape. This year the ancient little girl would have a surprise.

I needed reinforcements if my plan was to succeed. Everything would have to time out perfectly. Enlisting my father's help, we designated Christmas Eve as the appointed time. Under cover, we implemented "Operation Pony." My father visited with her in the living room while I stealthily, although not very quietly, maneuvered things into position in her dining room. To this day, I can't believe she didn't realize what was going on. I like to think she didn't know. Maybe she only pretended for my sake.

Later, as Dad helped her down the hall to her bedroom, I slid the plug into the socket. The warm glow of Christmas tree lights dispelled the gloomy darkness of the room. Beneath the tree were her gifts: a doll, a top, and a wooden pony on wheels. It might not be the pony of her dreams, but it was a pony all the same.

Early Christmas morning our phone rang. She never liked to talk on the phone, calling it the "instrument," so I was surprised to hear her voice.

"I got my pony," she said simply. "And a Christmas tree, too. Thank you."

The pony didn't live at her house for long. She died only a few years later when an especially mean strain of the flu made the rounds. She was ill for several days before she told anyone, and by then it was too late. Those in attendance at her bed granted her request and sang "Nearer My God to Thee" as she passed from this life to life eternal. Her last words were, "I can see Heaven, and it's glorious."

That little white-haired woman was my grandmother. My memories of her are as vivid and colorful as the beautiful patchwork quilts she made. Her influence on my life is deep and abiding, a subtle infusion of quiet hours spent together.

Never overly demonstrative or affectionate, she was not given to idle chatter. Many times when we were together, we would go for long periods without conversation. Time spent with her was a safe haven from the pressures in my world. Her house smelled of roses and an animal hide ottoman, a gift from her missionary son serving in Africa. Only the ticking of the mantle clock and the chirping of birds on the front porch punctuated the stillness and peace of moments spent in that place with her. She taught me the art of quilting. I can still picture her as she leaned in concentration over the panels. Her hands were twisted from arthritis but she could make the needle fly through the fabric.

On occasion, we discussed family members, her rose garden, or Scripture. Her well-worn Bible was always within easy reach. She didn't much care for the new translations of the Bible, but one day I shared a passage with her from *The Living Bible,* which had come alive to me. She listened skeptically before a tiny smile turned up the corners of her mouth.

"Thank you for sharing that with me," she said graciously. "That has meaning for me, too."

Many other women have influenced my life, but her calm assurance and strength are characteristics she passed along to me in the very depths of my being. I don't know if by genetics or by example, but I know her greatest strengths lie within me. I'm glad she celebrated one of her last Christmases on earth with a tree, a pony, and the joy of knowing how much I loved her.

A CHRISTMAS LESSON

SUZAN L. WIENER

The LORD is close to all who call on him,

yes, to all who call on him sincerely.

PSALM 145:18 NLT

"LOVE COMES
WHEN WE
TAKE THE
TIME TO
UNDER-
STAND AND
CARE FOR
ANOTHER
PERSON."

—*Janette Oke*

Being in a hospital on Christmas was hard enough, but when Christmas cards and decorative wreaths began to appear, I strangely felt even more alone. My belief in God had all but dwindled down to a fragment, and I felt empty. I had once been a very spiritual person. *Where was my family when I needed them the most?*

Tears wouldn't even flow. My eyes were dry, though my heart was breaking. The nurses tried to be friendly, as they could see how sad and lonely I was, and assured me I would be able to go home soon, but nothing seemed to help. They were even kind enough to share their presents of candy. But, even the staff humming carols didn't cheer me. The pain in my back was extremely excruciating, and I was constantly given medication which lulled me into a sedated sleep.

Christmas had always been a special time in my life. Our home was always filled with the holiday spirit and the love of family and friends. Our tree was cheerfully decorated with candy canes, snowflakes, and silver tinsel, but the memory was blurred by my twilight sleep.

My family was now scattered in different parts of the country, and I was totally alone. They called to see how I was doing; but with no visitations, it just wasn't the same, and my outlook was anything but positive. I couldn't even seem to pray because I felt like God had abandoned me.

Why, God, did You let this happen? I'm only forty, and now I feel like my life is over. The doctor had told me I couldn't return to work, and I had always enjoyed my job tremendously.

There was no answer from God at the moment, though there soon would be.

A woman was soon wheeled in that morning to share my room. She seemed to be suffering too, yet I found I had very little compassion for her. She slept most of the time, though once in a while I heard her praying.

Please, dear God, she said quietly, *help my friend in the next bed and give her comfort and peace.* She said it almost in a whisper, so I doubted God even heard her. And, *why,* I wondered, *would she pray for someone she didn't even know, whom she probably would never see again.*

When the acute pain was over, we began talking, slowly at first, but then we learned a lot about each other. She delighted in talking about her family most.

I learned that she had conquered cancer, heart trouble, and now she had a degenerative disc disease that might leave her paralyzed. That is just what I had also, but her faith gave her strength and courage. I hated to admit it, but I was envious that she had sustained her faith in God.

Christmas morning brought her entire family to our room—three daughters, husbands, and grandchildren. Her family's constant love seemed to heal her as much as her faith.

They included me in all their joy, as if I were a member of the family. Her granddaughter even embroidered a beautiful handkerchief just for me. It brought tears to my eyes. She seemed to forget her pain completely when they were with her, laughing and talking. Not for a moment did they neglect me, for which I was always grateful.

Every night when they went home, we prayed together. She offered prayers for me and eventually, I did the same for her. I began to have a warm, uplifted, and renewed feeling in my heart, even though I was still suffering. *Maybe things would be alright,* I hoped for both of us.

Somehow this gracious family had let me into their hearts, without asking for anything in return. She left the hospital a few days before me, but to my astonishment came back every day to visit me to see if I needed anything. We continued to pray for each other. She was looking much better, and I felt some better too.

The next week I was also able to go home, and I found that my belief in God had returned. I hadn't even realized it, until I suddenly felt like a new person, hopeful, happy, and even joyous. True, it wasn't my family who had been with me, but God had provided me with a family who was just as special and loving.

Now I know my belief in God will always be strong and never falter. In my deepest need, God blessed my life with a wonderful new friend, Katherine, and her loving family. And through them I experienced renewed hope and faith in my Heavenly Father who is always there. All we have to do is reach out to Him, and He will provide.

"MARY" CHRISTMAS

ESTHER M. BAILEY

Mary has chosen what is better, and it will not be taken away from her.

LUKE 10:42 NIV

"BRING YOUI
GIFTS TO
MARY'S SON
(RING THE
BELLS OF
CHRISTMAS)
GOD'S OWN
GIFT TO
EVERYONE;
BLESSED
CHILD OF
CHRISTMAS."

—*C.E. Macniven*

For a special event around Christmas, my friend Dottie ordered a cake from the bakery. "What name do you want on it?" the clerk asked.

"Well...just put Merry Christmas," Dottie said.

Imagine Dottie's surprise when she opened the box to see the words, "Mary Christmas."

After I laughed, I recalled many a Christmas where I had celebrated Christmas like Martha—and why not celebrate instead like Mary, "who sat at the Lord's feet listening to what he said" (Luke 10:39 NIV)?

For most of my life Martha influenced the way I prepared for Christmas. Shopping, wrapping gifts, cooking, decorating, and writing Christmas cards took top priority on my schedule. I was busy, busy, busy!

However, my priorities changed on December 1, 1999, when I underwent a mastectomy for Stage III advanced cancer. Even though I recovered quickly from the surgery, seasonal activities had lost their appeal.

After my surgery on Wednesday, I celebrated the second Sunday of Advent at church. Even the gymnasium where we worshiped at the time took on a sacred aura. I thought of things differently and in a brand-new light.

The service began with congregational singing of "Angels We Have Heard on High." Although often sung at Christmastime, the hymn held greater significance for me than ever before. If the angels had not brought the joyous news of Christ's birth, I would have had no direct access to God, no hope that He Himself would help me. And He had certainly been there for me through a very trying time in my life.

The sense of awe I experienced that day in church went home with me and stayed in my heart during the entire Christmas season. With serious thoughts on my mind, I spent considerable time in front of the nativity scene. I treasured the beautiful porcelain set because it represented friendship. The gift came from dear friends who were there for me from the time I learned of my cancer. God had answered our prayers, and I was sustained through the love of God and my dear friends. My heart swelled with joy as the bonds of friendship became even stronger—and more significant.

Since my bout with cancer, Christmas has never been quite the same. Instead of focusing on gifts, my focus has been on the Giver of new life. As I now send greetings to my friends, it is my hope to share meaning and purpose in life with them and the true glory of the Lord.

Celebrating the Advent season in ways promoted by the world can leave a void in the heart. Choosing to celebrate the meaning of the holiday promises everlasting rewards because the blessings received during a Christ-centered Christmas "will not be taken away" (Luke 10:42 NIV)—and, bring a renewed hope to the heart.

$\mathscr{M}$AKING IT REAL

DARLA SATTERFIELD DAVIS

I praise you, Father, Lord of heaven and earth,

because you have hidden these things from the

wise and learned, and revealed them to little children.

MATTHEW 11:25 NIV

"Away in a manger, no crib for His bed. The little Lord Jesus lay down His sweet head." My mother sang to me as she sat on the edge of my bed. She had a soft, sweet voice, and she adjusted her timing to help a five-year-old learn to follow along. She had just finished telling my brother and me the Christmas story, and then, spellbound, we bubbled with questions.

David had on his blue pajamas with cowboys on them, and I was clad in pink flannel. Our pajamas were warm and smelled laundry fresh and clothesline-dried; we had been bathed in warm frothy bubbles, sent to the bathroom, and had a drink;

"THE MOST VIVID MEMORIES OF CHRISTMASES PAST ARE USUALLY NOT OF GIFTS GIVEN OR RECEIVED, BUT OF THE SPIRIT OF LOVE, THE SPECIAL WARMTH OF CHRISTMAS WORSHIP, THE CHERISHED LITTLE HABITS OF HOME."

—*Lois Rand*

the same nightly ritual that was followed to the letter every night, rain or shine.

We were tucked in bed, and I could still taste Crest toothpaste in the corners of my mouth from brushing just before bedtime. Raggedy Ann was close beside me, and I knew we were moments away from our "Now I lay me down to sleep" prayer.

When my mother leaned over and "tucked my feet in tight" and bent to kiss me I didn't want to let go. Her hair was soft and shiny in the moonlight, and the smell of Breck™ shampoo filled my nose and made me want to hold on. "Good Night, Sleep Tight, Don't Let the Bedbugs Bite!" she said as she shut the door and left me and my brother alone in a bedroom we shared.

David fell asleep quickly, and I could hear his rhythmic breathing across the room. I began to think about poor baby Jesus and how His mother couldn't tuck Him in the way mine did. The more I thought about how cold it must have been out in an old stable, the sadder I felt. Hot tears filled my eyes when I thought about how upset Mary must have been to have to put her baby in a manger instead of a crib.

We were living in Washington at the time, and there was snow on the ground. Our little house didn't have a lot of heat either. I rolled back my heavy covers, climbed out of bed, and snuck into the living room where our Christmas tree stood dark in one corner of the room.

I went over and searched the tree until I found a little ornament that depicted the nativity in plastic and glitter. The tiny baby Jesus barely had a piece of painted cloth covering His midsection, and His little arms and legs were exposed. He couldn't have been more than a half-inch long, and the tiny dots painted for His eyes were slightly off center.

I could see my breath fogging a little silver glass bell on the branch above baby Jesus. I got up slowly and crept into the bathroom where I tore the tiniest corner off the toilet paper roll. I went back to the tree, folded the paper, and lay it carefully over Baby Jesus. Once I was satisfied that He would be warm, I went back to bed and buried myself deep in the covers.

My mother had told us the story of Jesus with such love and compassion that He became very real to me. She talked about His great love for us, and how He gave up Heaven to come here as a poor little baby in a manger. My mother loved Jesus, and she taught us to, as well. She shared how Mary and Joseph must have felt that night. Her words brought the shepherds and wise men to life as she told us their stories.

My earliest memories of Christmas are of my mother singing that song and telling me about baby Jesus. It was a story I recognized as very real, and it has followed me all my days. I have told this same story with much the same passion as my mother used many times to numerous children over the years. My prayer is always the same, *Please, Lord Jesus, help me make this story real in their hearts so they might love You, and follow You all of their days.*

The Christmas story is a story that will never be outdated and will never be told too many times. For it is when this story is told that we have given the greatest Christmas gift of all—Jesus, our precious Savior—to the world.

RIGHTS AND PERMISSIONS

MEET THE CONTRIBUTORS

Candy Neely Arrington has numerous published credits; she also co-leads the Writing 4 Him critique and instruction group and serves as a judge for the 2004 *Writers' Digest* book contest. She teaches youth discipleship and is a choir member at her church in Spartanburg, South Carolina. She and her husband have two teenage children.

Esther M. Bailey is a freelance writer with more than eight hundred published credits. She is co-author of two books: *Designed for Excellence* and *When Roosters Crow*. She resides in Phoenix, Arizona, with her husband, Ray. You can e-mail her at baileywick@juno.com.

Ginger Boda resides in Southern California, where she was born and raised. She has been married to her high school sweetheart, Mark, for twenty-seven years, with whom she raised three beautiful children. She loves to take photos and videos and capture her thoughts in poetry. She has had stories published in many inspirational venues, including write2theheart and Chicken Soup for the Bride's Soul.

Hugh Chapman and his wife, Julie, continue to teach in the Izard County School District in Brockwell, Arkansas. Hugh is a High School Business Education instructor and Julie teaches fourth grade. Their son, Dustin, is a second year Law student in Little Rock, and their daughter, Danielle, is a freshman at the University of Central Arkansas in Conway. You may e-mail Hugh and Julie at: Julchapman@yahoo.com.

Joan Clayton is the religion columnist for her local newspaper, and her newest release is a daily devotional. She has been included three times in *Who's Who Among America's Teachers*. She and her husband Emmitt reside in New Mexico.

Terrence Conklin is presently attending Dutchess Community College, where his area of study is music. He composes and performs original songs and appears in coffee houses throughout the community. In March of 2002, Terrence and his brother won first place in the Talent America contest in the "teen duo" category. He has recently begun to offer private instructions on the guitar.

Jay Cookingham is a freelance writer who is a featured writer on several websites, including www.fatherville.com, www.ibelieve.com, and www.christianwriters.com. His article, "Seven Promises from Your Husband" was featured on two separate occasions on Ken Canfield's syndicated radio program, "Today's Father." He also writes a monthly e-mail newsletter geared towards men. His latest projects include a book on fathering and co-authoring a book on parenting with his wife Christine. They have seven children blessing their home.

Martha Currington, a freelance writer and poet, lives in rural Alabama with her husband, Tom. She enjoys feeding and admiring the great variety of wild birds in the area. She has poetry published in eleven anthologies and other publishing credits include: Faith Writers Speak, Good Old Days Special (July 2003 issue), Purpose—a Christian Pamphlet, The Daily Mountain, which also featured her as a front page, "top story," and The Best of FaithWriters.com—Spring Edition.

Darla Satterfield Davis graduated from Southwestern Adventist University in north Texas, and has been teaching for fifteen years. She has been a contributor for *God's Way for Graduates, God's Way for Teachers,* and *Make Your Day Count for Teachers,* as well as several articles for local newspapers. Ms. Davis is an artist and the Owner/Steward of the Christian Fine Arts Center in Cleburne, Texas. She is available for speaking engagements throughout the summer months. You may contact Ms. Davis for more information at www.TheChristianFineArtsCenter.com.

David Flanagan is currently the Director of Business Development for Road to Responsibility, a nationally recognized organization based in Marshfield, Massachusetts that provides employment, housing, and recreation for the disabled. David has more than twenty years experience in community, government, and public affairs and is also a freelance writer. He and his wife, Linda, reside in Scituate, Massachusetts and have two sons Dave and Evan who certainly make life interesting and enjoyable. David may be reached at dflan14@aol.com.

Karen Majoris-Garrison is an award-winning author, whose stories appear in *Woman's World, Chicken Soup for the Soul,* and *God Allows U-Turns.* A wife and mother of two young children, Karen describes her family life as "heaven on earth." You may reach her at innheaven@aol.com.

Nancy B. Gibbs, the author of four books, is a weekly religion columnist for two newspapers, a writer for *TWINS Magazine,* and a contributor to numerous books and magazines. Her stories and articles have appeared in seven *Chicken Soup for the Soul* books, *Guideposts* books, *Chocolate for Women, Women's World, Family Circle, Decision, Angels on Earth, On Mission Magazine, Happiness,* and many others. Nancy is a pastor's wife, a mother, and a grandmother. She may be reached at daiseydood@aol.com or by writing P.O. Box 53, Cordele, GA 31010.

Jessica Inman loves reading and hopes it will make her a better writer. She also loves playing Frisbee with her dog Mack, running, and watching *Even Stevens.* She may be reached at jessinman03@yahoo.com.

Jennifer Johnson lives in Lawrenceburg, Kentucky, with her husband and three daughters. To write about Abba is her passion. Jennifer plans to teach middle school after completing her college degree.

Eva Juliuson was married eighteen wonderful years to her high school sweetheart, Steve, who passed into eternal life following an extended illness. There were many instances of "surprise" gifts from God during his courageous battle. The blessings continue in her life as she has now remarried, Dwight, and together they share seven children along with seven grandchildren and the knowledge that God's gifts never run out!

LaRose Karr is a church secretary and freelance writer in northeastern Colorado. Her work appears in the inspirational book series *God Allows U-Turns, The Upper Room,* and also in *The Quiet Hour* devotional guides. She believes her writing is a gift from God and gives Him all the glory. You may reach LaRose at rosiebay@kci.net.

Melinda Lancaster is an author and minister who resides in Spring Hill, Tennessee, with her husband, Greg, and son, Gregory. She is the co-founder of Don't Faint Ministries and has an extensive collection of inspirational writings online at www.jesusnotjunk.org. She enjoys speaking and ministering with music. Her hobbies include reading, listening to music, and writing poetry.

Kathryn Lay is a freelance writer of more than 850 articles, essays, and short stories for children and adults in hundreds of magazines and anthologies. She is the author of three books for children and youth, and also serves as a writing instructor.

Marcia Lee Laycock is a pastor's wife and mother of three girls. She has written articles for periodicals such as *Moody Monthly, Virtue,* and *Just Between Us,* as well as a weekly column, *The Spur* and many articles for newspapers across the country, including *Living Light News* and *Christian Week.* Marcia is an award-winning poet and fiction writer. While serving with Wycliffe Bible Translators in Papua, New Guinea, she wrote both radio and video scripts for the mission. She has also worked as the editor/writer for *Western Horizons,* a monthly publication of the Associated Gospel Churches of Canada. Marcia currently serves as president of Inscribe Christian Writers' Fellowship.

Patricia Lorenz is an internationally-known inspiration, art-of-living writer and speaker. She's one of the top contributors in the country to the *Chicken Soup for the Soul* books, with twenty stories in sixteen current *Chicken Soup* titles. She raised two daughters and two sons and has had kids in college every year for the past seventeen years. She lives in Wisconsin and loves her empty nest and the freedom to follow her dreams while she's still awake.

Barbara Marshak divides her time between novel writing and freelance work. With numerous articles published both regionally and nationally, she is currently pursuing publication for her first novel. Presently, Barbara is writing the biography of a Native American transformed from civil engineer to cultural role model and musical ambassador worldwide. Barbara resides in the Twin Cities with her husband and family.

Therese Marszalek is the author of *Breaking Out* (Publish America) and co-author of *Miracles Still Happen* (Harrison House). Her writing has appeared in numerous publications across the country. She is a columnist, inspirational speaker, and instructor for Christian Writers seminars in the Inland Northwest. She lives in Spokane, Washington, with her husband and their three children.

Janet Lynn Mitchell is a wife and mother of three. She is also an inspirational speaker and author of numerous articles and stories in compilations. Janet can be reached at Janetlm@prodigy.net or faxed (714) 633-6309.

Stefanie Morris has worked as a public relations professional in advertising and PR firms, nonprofits, and state government. She is actively involved in drama and children's ministries in her local church. She and her husband live in the countryside near Austin, Texas, with two dogs, two cats, four goats, one donkey, and roughly 100,000 honey bees! Her other hobbies include gardening and reading.

Amanda Pilgrim, Managing Editor for White Stone Books, resides in Tulsa, Oklahoma, with her husband, Mike, and their many animals. She enjoys spending any free time writing or volunteering at an exotic wildlife refuge in Broken Arrow. She has been a contributor for *Make Your Day Count for Teachers, God's Way for Graduates,* and *God's Way for Teachers.* Amanda can be contacted at mayflowerediting@cox.net.

Kayleen J. Reusser is a freelance writer who has published hundreds of articles for magazines and newspapers including *Today's Christian Woman, Decision, Business People, Whatzup!, Mature Years, Fort Wayne News-Sentinel and Journal-Gazette.* She also edits a newsletter for a jail chaplaincy program. Reusser is married and lives in the Midwest with her family.

Linda Rondeau resides in northern New York with her husband, Steve, a casework supervisor for Franklin County Department of Social Services. She is the author of more than twenty articles, stories, and poems. More of her work may be viewed at her website, www.lindarondeau.com.

Tonya Ruiz is a former international Ford fashion model and current pastor's wife. She has seen what the world has to offer and would rather have Jesus. She travels and speaks nationally on themes of true beauty, motherhood, marriage, and homeschooling. She has published her autobiography, *BeautyQuest: A Model's Journey,* and has contributed to numerous books.

Paula L. Silici is an award-winning author whose works of fiction, poetry, and nonfiction have appeared in both local and national publications. She is also a regular columnist for *Authorship, the National Writers Association,* a quarterly magazine for writers. Paula lives with her husband near Denver, Colorado. You can reach her at psilici@hotmail.com.

Laura L. Smith's growing list of publications includes *Cantaloupe Trees,* a children's chapter book (Publish America 2001) and short stories which appear in *God Allows U-Turns* (Barbour Publishing 2001) and *God Allows U-Turns, A Woman's Journey* (Barbour Publishing 2002). She lives in Oxford, Ohio, with her husband and two children.

Gloria Cassity Stargel is an assignment writer for *Guideposts Magazine;* a freelance writer; and author of *The Healing, One Family's Victorious Struggle with Cancer,* published originally by Tyndale House Publishers. *The Healing* has been re-released in special updated edition by Bright Morning Publications. Call 1-800-888-9529 or visit www.brightmorning.com.

Teena M. Stewart has worked in writing and editing for organizational newsletters and is a consultant/speaker with MinistryinMotion.net, a group that trains and equips leaders and volunteers to use their spiritual gifts and abilities for Christian ministry. She presently serves Northgate Christian Fellowship in Benicia, California, by teaching spiritual gifts/ministry discovery seminars and directing volunteer placement and equipping processes. You can contact Teena at teenastewart@teenastewart.com.

Anne Culbreath Watkins is the author of *The Conure Handbook* (Barron's Educational Series, Inc.). Her work has appeared in a wide variety of print publications such as *Angels on Earth, Bird Talk, Pet Age, The Front Porch, Whispers From Heaven,* and in numerous *Guideposts* books. She and her banjo-playing husband, Allen, live in rural Vinemont, Alabama where they love to spoil their grandchildren, Bailey, Chelsea, and Tyler.

Sharen Watson resides in Spring, Texas with Ray, her college sweetheart and "most supportive" husband of twenty-three years. They have one grown daughter and two teenage sons. Sharen is a freelance journalist, and writes short stories and allegories that find their root in the Word of God. She is currently working on her first book, dealing with women's issues. Sharen is also founder and director of *Words for the Journey Christian Writers Guild.* Her desire is that every word she writes will be a reflection of God's hope, restoration, and joy.

Suzan L. Wiener has had many published poems since she began writing fifteen years ago. She has been published in national magazines such as *Complete Woman, Modern Romances, True Confessions, True Story,* and *True Romance.* She also writes personal experience articles, as well as, anecdotes, jokes, and puns. You may reach Suzan at swiener1@tampabay.rr.com.

TELL US YOUR STORY

Can you recall a person's testimony or a time in your own
life when God touched your heart in a profound way?
Would your story encourage others to live God's Way?
Please share your story today, won't you?
God could use it to change a person's life forever.

For Writer's Guidelines, future titles, and submission
procedures, visit:
www.godswaybooks.com

Or send a postage-paid, self-addressed envelope to:
God's Way Editorial
6528 E. 101st Street, Suite 416
Tulsa, Oklahoma 74133-6754

This and other titles in the God's Way Series
are available from your local bookstore.

God's Way for Christmas
God's Way for Couples
God's Way for Fathers
God's Way for Graduates
God's Way for Mothers
God's Way for Teachers
God's Way for Teens
God's Way for Women

Visit our website at:
www.whitestonebooks.com

*"...To him who overcomes I will give some of the hidden manna to
eat. And I will give him a white stone,
and on the stone a new name written which
no one knows except him who receives it."*

REVELATION 2:17 NKJV

WHITE STONE BOOKS
LAKELAND, FLORIDA